FENG SHUI

Harmonizing Your Inner & Outer Space

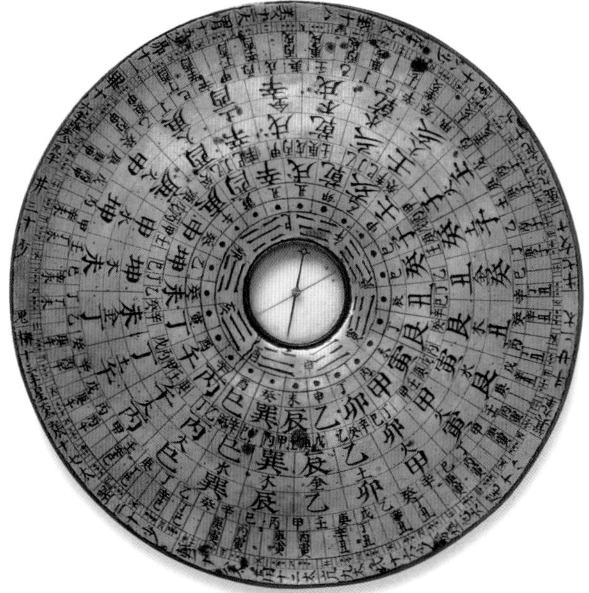

Zaihong Shen

Foreword by Stephen Skinner, publisher of *Feng Shui for Modern Living* magazine

A Dorling Kindersley Book

LONDON, NEW YORK, SYDNEY, DEHLI, PARIS MUNICH, and JOHANNESBURG

Project Editor and Photo Research/Editor: Barbara M. Berger
Book Designer: Scott Meola
Senior Art Editor: Mandy Earey
DTP Designer: Jill Bunyan
Production: David Proffit
Category Publisher: LaVonne Carlson
Art Director: Tina Vaughan
Cover Art Director: Dirk Kaufman
Editorial Consultant: Stephen Skinner
Developmental Editor: Stephanie Pedersen

First published in Great Britain in 2001 by Dorling Kindersley Limited 9 Henrietta Street, London WC2E 8PS

A CIP catalogue record for this book is available from The British Library

ISBN 0 7513 0864 1

Reproduced by Colourscan, Singapore
Printed and bound by
L. Rex Printing Company Limited, China

See our complete catalogue at
www.dk.com

CONTENTS

FOREWORD

There will be one of two possible questions on your lips as you pick up this book. You will be asking yourself "What is feng shui?" or alternatively, "Why yet another book on the subject?" Let me try to answer both of these questions, in reverse order.

There are now over 300 individual titles on feng shui, according to a recent search of amazon.com. Why would anyone need another? Well, back in 1976 when I wrote my first book on the subject, the only existing titles were in Chinese, in addition to several books written by nineteenth-century missionaries who primarily though of feng shui as a superstitious obstacle in their efforts to convert the Chinese to Christianity.

What they did not realize, and what the West has only begun to discover, is that feng shui is a mature body of real knowledge that the Chinese have been keeping to themselves for the last 3,000 years. Acupuncture and its attendant benefits only reached the West in the 1960s, and the amazing art of karate slightly earlier; feng shui was not known in the West until the 1980s and 1990s. Even by 1990 there were still only a few books in English on this fascinating tradition.

After a few serious books on feng shui appeared authors such as Derek Walters, Sarah Rossbach, and Evelyn Lip, the subject was partially "hijacked" by the New Age movement—which brought incense, spirituality, and color to the practice, introducing many elements that Chinese feng shui masters would not have recognized as part of their oeuvre. I am not one to decry the gradual and legitimate evolution of any theory, but in the case of feng shui, only a small fraction of the subject had by this time been unfolded before its whole essence began to change. In the 1990s writers like Lillian Too, Eva Wong, and more recently, Elizabeth Moran, brought more of the original feng shui to the West, in an organized manner.

In this present book Zaihong Shen examines feng shui through a cultural context. Although feng shui definitely has its roots in Taoism (Daoism), Ms. Shen relates it also to Buddhism and Confucianism. She approaches the subject from the point of view of its Chinese roots in the landscape, rather than simply as an adjunct to interior decorating. It is refreshing to read her analysis of soil types and weather, things you might not expect to find in a book on feng shui, but which are almost as central to feng shui as wind and water.

Feng shui has been defined as the "Art of Placement," but this restricts it to the furniture and furnishings within a home or office. Others have defined it in relation to ch'i, the subtle energy that flows through the land and affects our environment. But feng shui goes beyond these definitions. I prefer to think of it as nothing less

This feng shui practitioner is examining a *lo'pan* or feng shui compass while his aide takes notes.

than "luck engineering." For the ancient Chinese, luck was not synonymous with chance. Luck was opportunity. Of course, even if presented with opportunity many of us do not act and grasp it with both hands. Feng shui is for those of us who wish to do just that—grasp opportunity. For feng shui stirs up the subtle environment in such a way that more opportunities are attracted to the person who has improved his or her feng shui. For the Chinese, feng shui was Earth luck, the luck to be had by tapping the Earth's energies or ch'i. In some ways, the ancient Chinese discovery of feng shui is as significant as their discovery of paper-making, but this perception has yet to be spread in the West. This book's assistance in spreading the word about the importance of feng shui is more than welcome.

STEPHEN SKINNER
London
July 2000

INTRODUCTION

If you read popular magazines, watch television, surf the world wide web or even browse at your favorite bookstore, you are probably familiar with "feng shui," a term referring to the art and science of life-space design. Pronounced "fung schway," this ancient Chinese practice has become increasingly popular in the west as stress-plagued Americans, Canadians, and Europeans look for new ways to create harmony within their environments.

The purpose behind feng shui is to balance the energy or chi (also called ch'I or qi) in those places where we live and work. Pronounced "chee" and alternately called "vital energy," primal energy" and "the life force," chi is the fundamental energy found circulating around all things. According to feng shui, the design of our surroundings affects chi flow, and has a tremendous impact on our subconscious over time. For good health, serenity, peace of mind and even wealth, conception, and luck, this energy must circulate unimpeded throughout a person's environment. Yet severe angles, awkwardly placed doors and windows, various furniture placements, some color combinations and other factors can disrupt the constant, steady flow of this important energy.

Feng shui is not a one-size-fits-all, blanket approach to decorating a home or office. Feng shui is a practice that is tailored to each individual.

YIN, YANG, AND CHI

Yin and yang is a particularly Chinese concept, one that denotes the two opposing forces that exist within every living thing. While yin and yang is often explained simply as contrary energies, the principle is actually more complex: Everything contains and is balanced by its own mutually-dependent, polar opposites. The concept is symbolized by the sun and the moon—the two opposing forces active in our universe—and is often depicted as a two-toned circle. Within the dark half of the circle there is a small light dot, and within the light half lies a small dark dot. This suggests that, though opposites, there is a necessary relationship between yin and yang. Neither exists in and of itself. There is also the meaning of the words "yin" and "yang." In addition to "the moon" yin alternatively means "the dark side of a mountain," while yang means "the sun," or "the light side of a mountain."

While the concept may have been in China much longer, the term "yin and yang" wasn't created until late in the Zhou dynasty when philosophers were looking for a way to describe the way opposites depended on each other: There can be no light without darkness, or life without death.

According to these ancient philosophers, yin and yang is an always-changing combination. Day gives way to night, something hot can grow cold, someone outgoing can become self-protective, the living eventually die. According to Chinese thought, this constant flux is a good thing. It is what creates chi or the life giving force of the universe.

Beijing's Forbidden City, shown above, was built in the 15th century according to feng shui theory.

For instance, a skilled feng shui practitioner first analyzes a person's birth chart, an intricately-detailed maze of zodiac signs, triagram charts, elemental charts, star combinations, phases, annual numbers and other divining tools—maybe also requesting this information of all individuals living or working in a certain space. Since each human in born in a specific time in which the universe was positioned in a specific position, the Chinese believe that one's character, health, career, luck, family and even future can be determined by his or her time of birth. After studying the birthchart, the practitioner examines any special needs or quirks this person might have, then studies the person's physical environment. Finally, these elements are considered together and various solutions are recommended to balance the space's chi.

However, one can successfully practice feng shui without a practitioner—all that's needed is common sense. Feng Shui was created through common sense and still works as common sense. For instance, if you move your bed to a lucky direction then find yourself getting headaches from sleeping this way, reposition your bed! If you shift your desk to face a more auspicious direction then find yourself unable to get anything done, move the desk back to its previous position. For those who do want some type of help, visiting an interior designer or architect is an option. These professionals usually have a strong eye for space, colors, light and materials. Though few are trained in feng shui, most have a knowledge of visual flow and proportion, two concepts used in feng shui.

Today, feng shui is most often associated with balancing a space's energy, but the practice was born of necessity. Feng shui literally means "wind water," words the ancient Chinese used to symbolize the two major forces of nature. Indeed, over 6,000 years ago, feng shui meant finding a sheltered location that was free from wind (feng) and with abundant water (shui). Many of the earth's early humans believed the world was filled with spirits and deities, some kind and some malicious. The ancient Chinese were no exception. They believed powerful spirits lived within animals, plants, rocks, minerals, waters, thunder, lightening and weather. Like other early people, the ancient Chinese relied on local shamans to help keep capricious deities happy. In fact, it was common for villagers to ask shamans for advice on where to build a home or tomb, how to situate a temple, when and where to plant crops and other topics that could potentially displease the spirits.

Interestingly, although the practice of feng shui has been around for six thousand years or more, the term "feng shui" is relatively recent. It was

I CHING, FENG SHUI & SCIENCE

Feng shui, Taoism, qi gong, astrology—these are just a few of the Chinese disciplines based on the *I Ching* (Yijing).

Of the disciplines rooted in the I Ching, only feng shui has continuously evolved through Chinese history. From its beginnings 6000 years ago to the present, feng shui theories have been set up, tested, either abandoned or accepted, and developed. Much of feng shui's "fine-tuning" has occurred in the last few centuries as technology presented such advances as mirrors, electricity, indoor plumbing, telephones, elevators, and computers, and more was learned about the environment and science. In fact, in China, feng shui is considered interrelated to the following disciplines:

Astrology	Astronomy
Ecology	Geography
Geology	Meteorology
Psychology	

The above list may grow longer in the near future. After all, Feng Shui theory will continue to change as humankind's knowledge expands and our world changes.

USING FENG SHUI

Feng shui is used primarily in determining the following:

A Comfortable Location. Feng shui can help locate a building that benefits a person's health, career, wealth, luck and family. Note that for some people, increasing one's benefits may require moving to a different home or apartment building, or even relocating to a different city, state, country, or cultural environment.

A Building's Relationship with the Environment. By helping you locate and adjust the orientation, shape, entrance, road and exterior factors of a house, apartment or business, feng shui can help you find a location that is auspicious for you, your family or your company.

A Building's Relationship with Humans. The interior design of a house or apartment has great influence on a person's health and luck. Factors that can help or hinder the flow of chi include furniture placement, decorating materials and color schemes.

first used in the fourth century A.D. in a test called Book of Burial which explained the relationship between the earth and qui. Directly before this, the practice was called Kan Yu—Kan meaning "heaven's way" or "the study of the universe," and Yu meaning "earth's way" or "the study of earth." It was also known as the Qing Wu Method, roughly translated as "the way of the sun and earth."

FENG SHUI & HUMAN LIFE

An ancient Chinese saying about good fortune says: "First comes destiny, then comes luck. Third comes feng shui, followed by philanthropy and education." Indeed, both the ancient and modern Chinese believe there are several things one can do to increase one's luck. The following list contains a number of elements believed to influence good fortune:

Fate
Many Chinese people believe that the year you were born in is the most accurate determiner of your fate; The birth month plays a slightly diminished role, the day a slightly more diminished role, and the hour an even more diminished role.

Opportunity
Every time you make choices you influence your luck. In fact, the Chinese believe that each subsequent opportunity that arises in your life is determined by the one before it.

Feng Shui
Your home's interior and exterior environment can bring positive or negative chi.

Doing good things for next life
Performing good deeds for the people around you is believed to ensure good things in your next life. Plus, when you are kind to others, they are kind in return—an easy way to increase your luck!

Studying
Accumulating knowledge opens a person's inner senses, which in turn will direct an individual to his or her life's correct direction.

Another Chinese theory developed by Taoists to help people understand how to manage their life advises that "Timing is from heaven, location is on earth, and harmony is of people."

Timing
The Chinese believe that human fate is controlled by the universe. Because the universe is constantly evolving, each person's fate is always changing. Thus, a person born lucky may become unlucky in middle or old age, while a person born unlucky may become lucky later in life. In other words, your luck depends on the time, or the position of the universe.

Location
In the West, we have the saying "Location, Location, Location." While this is refers to business real estate, it is just as relevant to other areas of life. For instance, being in an area where there is a fault line is an unlucky location when an earthquake occurs.

People
The Chinese believe the people you allow into your life bring their good or bad luck with them, making it is important to select your friends carefully. In general, individuals with high morals are seen as more beneficial as friends than those with poor morals.

閑來隱几枕書眠夢入
壺中別有天彷彿希
夷親面目大還真訣得
親傳晋昌唐寅為
東原先生寫圖

PART ONE

ROOTS OF FENG SHUI

CHAPTER 1

CHINESE CULTURE AND RELIGION

FOR THE LAST 6,000 YEARS SOME FORM OF LIFESPACE DESIGN HAS BEEN PRACTICED IN CHINA.

ROOTS OF FENG SHUI

Long before the discipline developed into what we now call feng shui, ancient tribal Chinese were carefully aligning graves according to the stars: neolithic Chinese burial sites from this time have been found, each grave with its head facing south. The south has always been considered an auspicious direction in feng shui, because the south-facing ground provides the "breath of cosmic life." Chinese believe the dead need chi energy. A lack of this cosmic breath could adversely affect the fortune of the person's descendants: if the dead souls are happy, they will ensure that the living souls of descendants

ROOTS OF CHINESE CULTURE

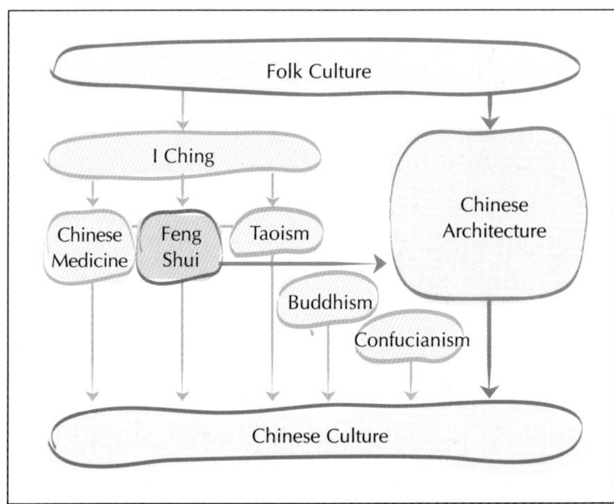

Chinese culture is an amalgam of ancient folk traditions; feng shui and medical theory; and three major religions.

are happy. Furthermore, each grave was rounded at the head and squared at the body's feet. In Chinese symbology the sky is round and the earth is square.

In addition to orienting houses for the dead (yin houses), early feng shui was used to situate houses for the living (yang houses). Indeed, it is in the planning of individual residences that feng shui is most strongly rooted in the practical. The ancient Chinese noticed that a house was warmer and more protected when facing the sunny south and surrounded by rolling hills to dissipate any harsh winds. Such a site became known as the "Dragon Protecting the Pearl" in ancient texts and it was said that here chi could gather and grow instead of being swept away by wind. Conversely, an area with strong winds was not a good feng shui site as the chi would dissipate, carrying away the good luck and wealth with it.

In ancient China, feng shui was not an esoteric discipline practiced only by certain tribal members—it was an integral part of native culture, something that touched everyone's life. As proof of this, feng shui scholars point to archeological evidence showing that the neolithic Chinese routinely build encampments and villages inside the bows of rivers. This lucky position was—and still is—thought to provide a healthy flow of chi.

FENG SHUI IN HISTORY
This painting from the Qing Dynasty (AD 1644-1912) depicts a feng shui practitioner and his aides searching for an auspicious building site.

Indeed, the development of Chinese culture is reflected in feng shui. Throughout the development of the human civilization, new philosophies were combined with lifespace placement, beginning with astrology, astronomy and mathematics, which supplied intricate star charts designed to help rulers, farmers and even peasants build palaces, public buildings, graveyards, farms and residences. The *I Ching* contributed detailed triagrams and maps to feng shui practice. The three primary religions of China—Taoism, Buddhism, and Confucianism—also added their imprint to feng shui.

TAOISM

LAOZI
Taoism, founded by Laozi in the sixth century BC, was the first religion to incorporate feng shui theory.

Before Taoism was founded in ancient China, there were shamans who lived in harmony with their natural environment. These shamans often dwelled in mountain hideaways and served local communities by interpreting omens, predicting weather cycles and serving as spiritual links between local populations and invisible spirit worlds. According to legend, shamans could control forces of nature, travel beneath the ground and through mountains, and visit the stars. In addition to these mythic abilities, the ancient shamans of China were responsible for ancient Chinese sciences such as astronomy. They also developed meditation systems and energy circulation exercises which later became known as chi kung (qi gong). It was out of this shamanistic tradition that Taoism was born.

Taoism is attributed to a philosopher named Laozi (also known as Li Erh or Lao Tzu) who lived during the Chou Dynasty (around 580 BC). An officer of the royal library, upon his death Laozi was said to have become a dragon.

After years of study he became enlightened and decided to retreat from society, traveling to far Western China on a water buffalo. Upon reaching a distant mountain pass, Laozi met the Keeper of the Pass, Wen-Shih. Wen-Shih convinced Laozi to record his insights in what became known as the Tao Te Ching (also called the Dao De Jing). This book of philosophy is a kind of manual of self-transformation and meditation written about the Tao or Dao (which means "the way"). Laozi was aided by his student, a philosopher named Zhuangzi. The two developed a spirituality based on ancient nature worship. In fact, a basic tenet of Taoism is the order and harmony of nature, which is considered more stable and enduring than the power of any human government or institution constructed by humans. Early Taoists were especially enthusiastic supporters of *wu wei*. Roughly translated as "no action", this approach taught that art and life followed the creative path of nature—not the values of human society.

TAOIST MOUNTAINS

☯ Considering the high esteem Taoism had for nature, perhaps it is not surprising that China's first Taoists chose mountains as holy sites to mediate and practice their religion. It was widely believed that in the mountains, religious energy was isolated and less disturbed by outside energy.

☯ When choosing religious mountains, the Taoists were not concerned with dramatic shapes or size—what they were after was mountains with rich soil, flourishing plant life, a healthy animal population, and a climate with enough moisture and sun. This mix signaled a perfect balance between yin and yang energy, which Taoists believed was necessary for physical and spiritual well-being.

If there is one Taoist belief most strongly associated with feng shui, it is this: Nature is the ultimate power and humans, as part of nature, benefit by following natural laws. Because nature is perfectly balanced, a house or other structure can cause imbalance unless carefully placed. Living out of balance with nature eventually affects humankind. Modern day feng shui practitioners point to depleted ozone layer, global warming, over-fished oceans and the depletion of soil as warnings of what can happen when we live at odds with nature.

TAOSIM'S NINE HEALING ARTS

Taoism placed such a strong emphasis on the life-prolonging power of good health that the religion espoused the following nine healing arts:

I. Meditation
Daily meditation helps a person stay centered by aligning body, breath and mind. Specific meditations are sometimes referred to as Inner Alchemy, or the path to enlightenment and immortality.

II. Nutrition
The Chinese combine food and prescribe diets based on the energetic qualities of food and the specific needs of the individual.

III. Movement Arts
Taoist movement arts include chi kung (qi gong), tai chi, and martial arts, which are used to train both the physical and energetic bodies. The first three healing arts—meditation, nutrition and movement arts—are known collectively as the "Three Pillars of Health."

IV. Herbal Medicine
According to Chinese herbal medicine, every herb has an energetic quality that can be used to heal a specific symptom or illness.

V. Acupuncture
Acupuncture is the stimulation of specific points along the body with needles. Related to acupuncture is acupressure, where the same points are stimulated with finger pressure, herbs or heat.

VI. Feng Shui
According to ancient Chinese beliefs, all natural geographical structures have energy. Feng shui is the science of maximizing natural positive energy by strategic placement. It allows people to exist harmoniously with the earth.

VII. The Yin and Yang Method (The Art of the Bedchamber)
Sexual energy can be harnessed and cultivated for both longevity and spiritual growth. The yin and yang method encourages health and healing through male and female energies, which are exchanged during intercourse.

VIII. Divination
Divination is the art of seeing and interpreting signs. More specifically stated, the Chinese believed that in everything, the microcosm is a mirror of the macrocosm. Thus, a healing system such as reflexology uses the palm, foot, ear, scalp, or face to treat a disease located elsewhere in the body.

IX. Bodywork
Chinese bodywork is used to encourage the efficient flow of energy through throughout the body. This bodywork includes various forms of massage and soft tissue manipulation (Tui Na),acupressure (Anmo), and internal organ massage (Chi Nei Tsang).

BUDDHISM

BUDDHIST TEMPLE
Many Buddhist temples incorporate feng shui theory in their design and placement; this mountain lake site has ideal chi.

Though Buddhism played an important role in ancient China, the religion was founded in Northern India in the sixth century BC by Siddhartha Gautama, who became known as the Buddha (Enlightened One). The Buddha achieved enlightenment (Nirvana) through meditation and established a community of monks to follow his example and encourage others. Buddhism teaches that Nirvana can be reached through meditation and good moral and religious behavior. It also maintains that people are reincarnated and that their lives are happy or sad depending on their actions (karma) in a previous life. Buddhist belief is centered around the Four Noble Truths: that all living beings must suffer, that desire and self-importance cause suffering, that the achievement of Nirvana ends suffering, and that Nirvana can be attained through meditation and righteous actions, thoughts and attitudes.

Unlike Confucius, Buddha preached respect, love, and eternal salvation for not only men but for women, gods, and animals. Buddhist monks were further commanded not to harm any living creature—the reason vegetarianism is so strongly associated with Buddhism. In addition, Buddhism encourages four modes of inner conduct: loving-kindness, compassion, sympathetic joy, and equanimity toward the impure and evil.

While there are many different types of Buddhism, Zen Buddhism is the type prevalent in China. In fact, the name "Zen" is derived from the Chinese *Chan'an-na*, which is a corruption from the Buddhist *Dhyana*, meaning "meditation." According to legend, Buddhism entered China circa AD 600, when a monk named Bodhi-Dharma introduced it to China. It didn't become popular until nearly a century later when Chinese Taoist, philosopher and theologian, Hui-neng, who died in AD 713, established Zen as a sect of Buddhism.

Because Buddhism was established in China after Taoism, and because it was popularized by feng shui-practicing Taoists, most Buddhist schools honor feng shui tenets. Many Buddhist temples and other structures are built according to feng shui

principles. For example, temples face south and contain "layers" of space, including a pleasure garden, an outer door, a vestibule and several inner doors. Interestingly, Buddhism also shaped feng shui, most notably in the arena of death. Before Buddhism, most Chinese believed the dead existed as spirits that could bring harm or good luck to the living. By the time of the Ming Dynasty (AD 1368-1644), Buddhism's belief in reincarnation had affected the concept of grave design. In addition to simply facing graves south, elaborate burial chambers were built using five to ten layers of different types of soil and baked clay to keep out moisture, grave robbers, and animals—this protected the body's soul until it was able to move into to its next life.

During the Ming Dynasty, Taoist and Buddhist monks devoted much energy to studying and perfecting feng shui principles. Interestingly, it was the work of these monks that led people to associate feng shui with Taoism and Buddhism. Feng shui principles became so strongly interwoven with the two religions that lifespace design was seen less as part of Chinese native culture and more as a religious practice. Even today, many Chinese still view feng shui as a religious practice instead of a scientific discipline.

BUDDHIST MOUNTAINS

- Early Chinese Buddhists looking for a secluded area to practice their religion, constructed temples in what are now know as China's four major Buddhist Mountains. Isolated and quiet, these mountains are larger and showier in shape than their Taoist counterparts, and were chosen with less regard toward soil quality, plant life and animal diversity. Buddhists favored these mountains for their strong yang energy, while Taoist looked for mountains with a perfect balance of yin and yang energy.
- Other differences between Taoists and Buddhists include the kind of temples each religion favored. The Buddhists built large, eye-catching temples at or near the top of their mountains, where the energy was its strongest; the Taoists not only built temples on the sides of mountains where the energy was more balanced, they were careful to create inconspicuous structures that blended with the environment.

THE BUDDHIST WAY

Like Taoism's *Tao Te Ching* and Confucianism's *Book of Analects*, Buddhism's Dhamapada is a text of religious wisdom designed to help followers practice and maintain their faith. Composed of short proverbs, the *Dhamapada* offers easy-to-understand lessons. Here are a few selections:

- All that we are is the result of what we have thought: is founded on our thoughts and is made up of our thoughts.
- As a solid rock is not shaken by the wind, so the wise man does not waver before blame or praise.
- There is an old saying: they blame him who sits silent; they blame him who speaks much; they blame him who says little. There is no one in the world who does not get blamed.
- All animals and humans tremble at punishment and all beings fear death; remember that you are like them and do not kill nor cause slaughter.

CONFUCIANISM

Confucianism was started by Chiu Kong, who was also called Kong the Philosopher, or K'ung-fu'-tse. Confucius, as he is known today, lived in the sixth and fifth centuries BC. He emphasized the importance of *li* (proper behavior), *ren* (sympathetic attitude) and *hsiao* (ancestor worship)—all tenets that remain important in modern China.

Since its beginning, Confucianism has been intertwined with Taoism. Laozi (Lao Tzu), the founder of Taoism, is often regarded as one of Confucius' early mentors. And while the Confucian tradition served as the ethical and religious foundation of many ancient Chinese institutions, elements of Taoism—such as chi kung (qi gong), feng shui, herbal medicine and the belief of yin and yang—offered a range of alternatives and embellishments to Confucian beliefs. For the majority of Chinese, there was no choosing between Confucianism and Taoism. Except for a few strict Confucians and Taoists, the vast majority of Chinese subscribed to elements of both religions—and in modern China, Confucianism is considered more of a philosophy than a religion.

CONFUCIUS

Confucius's ideals influenced feng shui in the areas of design and placement that stressed leadership and familial hierarchy.

Confucius's audience was largely limited to the rulers and aristocrats for whom he worked. At 19 he entered the service of a noble family as superintendent of parks and herds. At 32 he was asked to teach ancient rituals to a minister's sons. At 33 he went to Lo-yang, the imperial capital, to study the customs and traditions of the Chou Empire, which by then had split into numerous warring states of various sizes, and whose capital remained solely a religious center. On this occasion Confucius is said to have visited Laozi, the founder of Taoism. When Confucius was 34, the prince of Lu was threatened by powerful rivals among the local nobility and forced to flee. Confucius accompanied him to a neighboring state. At the age of 51 he returned to political life, working as minister of justice and finally as an advisor to the king of Lu.

Confucianism began circulating among the elite during the Han dynasty (207 BC–AD 220), and in the Sung dynasty (AD 960–1279) it became an official state religion. It was during this time that the doctrine grew into a system for the training of officials and public schools were replaced with Confucian schools.

Feng shui is not closely associated with Confucianism. In fact, the strongest affiliation between the two disciplines occurs in the context of Confucianist ancestor worship. Since burials represent a way to show respect, feng shui is used to orient and create graves. Also, Confucius's theories of hierarchy were utilized by dynastic emperors who declared that no one but they could live in structures that faced perpendicularly south to north; his patriarchal ideals influenced the design of family homes.

CONFUCIUS SAY

Confucius was well known for his teaching style, which revolved around short fables proclamations. Although Confucianism has declined in importance in China since the communist revolution, its estimated five million followers can find spiritual lessons in *The Book of Analects* (Lun Yu), from which the following bits of wisdom are collected:

- Sorrow not because men do not know you; but sorrow that you do not know men.
- When you know a thing, maintain you know it; when you do not, acknowledge it. This is the characteristic of knowledge.
- To see what is right and not to do it, that is cowardice.
- The superior man is not contentious. He contends only as in competitions of archery; and when he wins he will present his cup to his competitor.
- He who has sinned against Heaven has none other to whom his prayer may be addressed.
- Tell me, is there anyone who is able for one whole day to apply the energy of his mind to virtue? It may be that there are such, but I have never met with one.
- It is as hard to be poor without complaining as to be rich without becoming arrogant.
- The superior men are sparing in their words and profuse in their deeds.
- Confucius was asked, "What say you of the remark, 'Repay enmity with kindness'?" And he replied, "How then would you repay kindness? Repay kindness with kindness, and enmity with justice."
- I have not yet met the man who loves virtue as he loves beauty.
- Not to react after committing an error is in itself an error.

CHAPTER TWO

UNDERSTANDING FENG SHUI THEORY

BEFORE THE THEORY OF RELATIVITY, BEFORE THE DISCOVERY OF BACTERIA AND VIRUSES, BEFORE SCIENCE WAS USED TO TRACK WEATHER SYSTEMS, AND EVEN BEFORE COMPASSES WERE COMMON, PEOPLE USED OBSERVATION TO EXPLAIN THE WORLD.

FENG SHUI METHODS

In ancient China observations about climate, geography, star systems, and human health led to the creation of such theories as chi, yin and yang, the five elements, I Ching, and pa qua. It was from these ancient ideologies that feng shui developed.

Like many theories, early feng shui supported diverging interpretations and different methods—two of these systems are still used today. The first, and easiest to learn, is called the Form School (*Hsing Fa*). Hsing Fa was formed in Jiang Xi province. It is the oldest system, said by some to date back to the Chin dynasty (AD 300). Initially its purpose was to orient tombs, for even before Taoism, Buddhism, and Confucianism, ancestor worship played an important part in Chinese life. Later, Form School feng shui was used to orient homes according to surrounding geography, water availability, and weather patterns. An intuitive approach, Form School uses analysis, common sense, and perception to create lucky placements.

A slightly younger and more complicated type of feng shui is the Compass School (*li fa*). Developed in the Fujian province, it is rooted in the idea that each of the eight cardinal directions (north, northeast, east, southeast, south, southwest, west, northwest) exert a different energy. This type of feng shui was so-named because it relies on a compass. A south-pointing compass was used by

CHI KUNG IS THE WAY TO MANAGE THE CHI INSIDE YOUR BODY. FENG SHUI IS THE WAY TO MANAGE THE CHI OUTSIDE YOUR BODY, IN THE ENVIRONMENT.

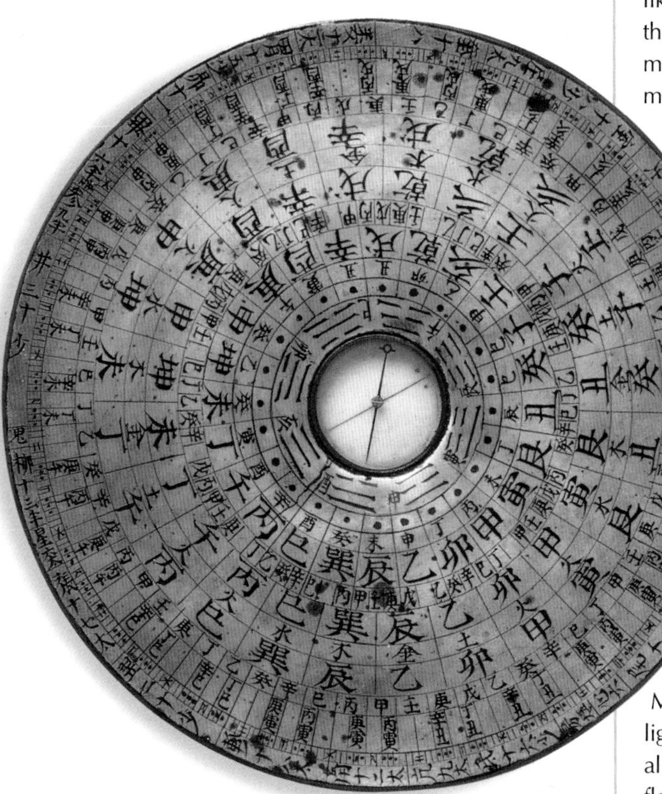

LO P'AN COMPASS
The development of feng shui spurred the invention of this instrument that helps calculate Compass School orientations.

early Chinese practitioners; now called a *lo p'an* compass, it is still used today by many modern practitioners. Li fa is not an intuitive approach, but a mathematical method that utilizes direction, astronomy, astrology, and numerology.

THE ENERGY OF MATTER

In early China, chi was believed to be an invisible gas or vapor that surrounded the world. The concept slowly developed into what we today know as chi: an invisible energy that moves fast or slow, strong or feebly—depending on the situation—over the earth and through our bodies. Yet, modern-day Chinese also consider chi as the substance comprising solid matter. If this sounds like a far-out concept, consider Albert Einstein's theory of relativity, which states that energy equals mass times the velocity of light—in other words, mass is simply a form of energy. Asked to explain how he came up with his theory, Einstein said "It followed from the special theory of relativity that mass and energy are both but different manifestations of the same thing — a somewhat unfamiliar conception for the average mind. Furthermore, the equation $e=mc^2$—in which energy is put equal to mass, multiplied by the square of the velocity of light—showed that the mass is formed by large amounts of energy. But the energy contained in mass is usually active in minor levels that equipment cannot test but can be 'felt' by human intuition."

While feng shui masters specialize in analyzing matter's energy, they are not the only individuals able to feel an object's chi. Mountains, rocks, lakes, as well as walls, floors, lighting fixtures, furniture, and knick-knacks—these all qualify as matter. When an architect says a floorplan "does not feel right" or an interior decorator claims there is something about a room that "just doesn't work," he or she has located an energy imbalance within a home's matter and is searching for a way to analyze that imbalance. And who hasn't had the experience of walking into a house or apartment and feeling completely at home, or listening to a new homeowner explain that she bought a certain home because it "just felt right"? All these are examples of matter's chi.

FORM SCHOOL (HSING FA)

The Form School studies the relationship between forms. Originally, the discipline studied the placement of homes, villages, public buildings, and graves in relation to geographical factors, including mountains, water, soil, and ground coverage. These factors became fundamental guidelines for centuries of hsing fa practitioners. While they continue to play an important role in modern day feng shui, they have been joined by other, often man-made structures. Analyzing the relationship between natural and man-made shapes allows a feng shui practitioner to orient a building to receive healthy chi. This also allows him or her to indicate auspicious building shapes, materials, colors, landscaping, and more. The next six pages explore important considerations within the Form School.

Feng shui experts believe that a dragon mountain can affect both surrounding and distant homes with its strong chi.

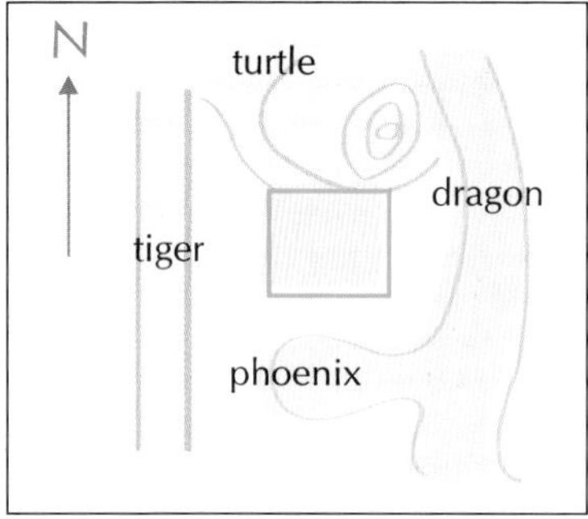

Hsing Fa teaches that the most divine earthly site has a dragon (low, long mountains) to the east, a tiger (tall peaks) to the west, a turtle (tall mountain) to the north and a phoenix (flat land or water) to the south.

DRAGON MOUNTAINS

The Chinese's reverence toward mountains is rooted in practicality: Mountains help shield an area from strong winds—which can blow away good chi—while their southern slopes help retain and diffuse the sun's warmth. However, not all mountains are auspicious: Those with sheer faces, steep precipes, sharp angles, a larger proportion of rock to soil, or a lack of wildlife, are considered to harbor negative chi.

The most auspicious Chinese mountains and hills are called Dragon Mountains. The ancient dragon was simply an auspicious snake, yet after the Han Dynasty (207 BC– AD 220) the animal became the symbol of Chinese culture and was "updated" with the body of a snake, scales of a fish, head of a horse, horn of a kirin (a mythologized horned mammal), and the jaw of an eagle. In the Form School, the dragon

DRAGONS, TIGERS, TURTLES, AND PHOENIX

In ancient Chinese mythology, the dragon, tiger, turtle, and phoenix were celestial animals, each associated with a specific landform. The ultimate goal of early feng shui masters was to find a valley protected by these four celestial animals, for that land was said to be a place of heaven on earth. (In ancient China, because the south was denoted as the top-center direction on maps and compasses, this concept was often phrased as "a dragon to the left, a tiger to the right, a turtle at the bottom and a phoenix at the top.")

In feng shui, the dragon—also known as the green or blue dragon—refers to a long, undulating mountain chain or human-made structure. The dragon represents east, spring, green, and yang.

The tiger, or white tiger, is a chain of mountains or a human-made structure that is taller than the dragon mountains, yet not as long. The tiger was at one time common in Western China, which is why it represents the west. It also symbolizes autumn, white, and yin. Interestingly, a small number of feng shui practitioners believe that the dragon mountains should be taller than the white tiger mountains.

You may hear the turtle referred to as the black or dark turtle. A symbol of steady power in China (its shell was used in ancient northern divination), the turtle symbolizes north, winter, black, and yin. While some feng shui masters claim that the height of a turtle mountain or building does not matter, other feng shui masters say the turtle's peaks must be higher than the tiger's.

What is now called the phoenix was known in ancient China as the crimson or red bird, an animal originally modeled after the common sparrow. Because of the larger amount of birds toward China's tropical south, the phoenix represents south, as well as summer, red, and yang. This is the flattest of the landforms and need not be elevated at all. In fact, the most common phoenix forms in ancient china were a body of water, such as a stream or large pond. In modern times, the phoenix can be represented by a road or lane.

symbolizes strong, balanced energy—so strong in fact that a dragon mountain's chi is said to affect the mountains, hills, and other landforms around it. This is why a dragon mountain is considered in feng shui analysis to affect faraway structures.

According to the teachings of the Form School, dragons are not found on flat land or in steep mountains, but reside in favorable elevated sites where the mountain chain is old and stable with a generous amount of rich soil. The chi in such a site is said to be luckier than the aggressive energy found in a newer, bigger, and steeper mountain chain—which most likely has less vegetation and, because of it's younger age, less abundant soil. Wherever a dragon formation is found, there will also be a tiger formation (see the "Dragons, Tigers, Turtles, and Phoenix" sidebar above).

WATER

In times before indoor plumbing and outdoor sprinkler systems, a nearby source of running water was deemed essential for human health and for agriculture. Because running water was also considered to carry chi, a river or stream was considered an important source of fresh energy. In this century, few people live near creeks, streams, rivers, or other natural bodies of water; today, roads, avenues, streets, lanes, sidewalks, and other artificial waterways are considered the modern chi-moving equivalent of running water. In feng shui theory, a very slow-moving river or stream represents stagnant chi, a situation that the Chinese believe can cause fatigue and lowered immune system function. From a scientific standpoint, stagnant water can be dangerous because it can host malaria-causing mosquitoes, different types of biting insects, and accelerate the growth of bacteria. Water that moves too swiftly, however, is said to carry good fortune

The embracing shape of the river provides the inhabitants of this peninsula with a safe, protected environment that will accumulate chi and prosperity.

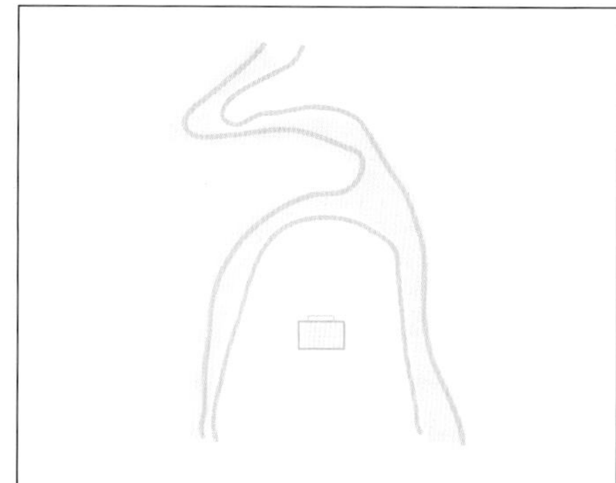

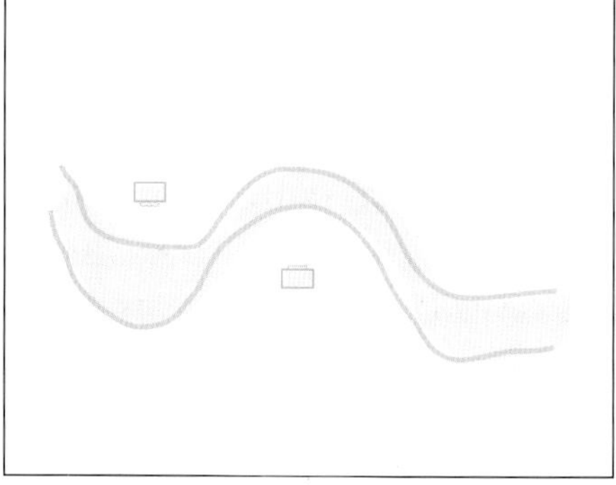

A site inside the bow of a moderately-moving waterway is considered a chi-enhancing position.

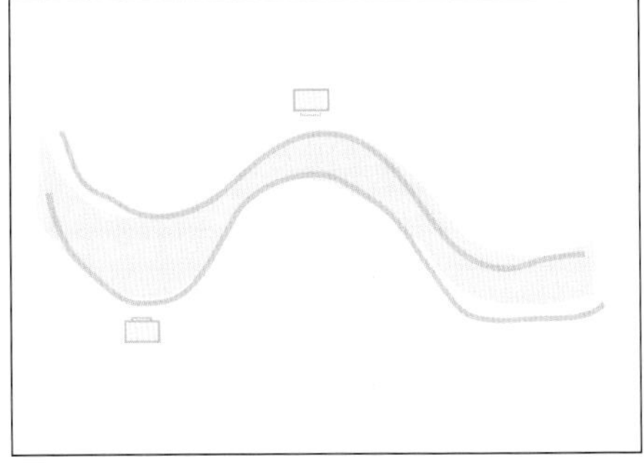

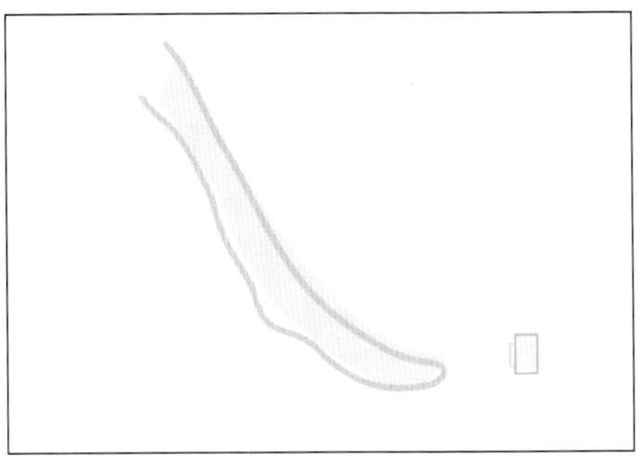

Building on the outer bank of a waterway's bend or at the tip of its delta is considered both dangerous—a rise in the river's water level can flood a home or settlement—and chi-sapping.

A waterway that is moderately fast and deep is auspicious, yet structures such as this that are built on an outer bank risk sacrificing their chi in the event of a flood.

away from a site. From a practical standpoint, a fast-moving current represents a danger to anyone who happens to be near the water.

According to feng shui theory, the ideal shape for a river, stream, or other body of running water is not straight—which carries fortune-giving chi too quickly away from a site—but meandering (preferably meandering away from a chi-rich mountain water source). Bows in a river have historically been considered propitious places to build homes, because the house or village is cradled in a semi-circle of lucky chi. Today, roads are given the same consideration as waterways, meaning it is luckier to live alongside a curved road, sidewalk, or driveway, than alongside a straight passageway (see pages 90-91).

In practical terms, a river's depth indicates its usefulness. A moderately deep or deep river has enough water to continuously supply several farms, while a shallow river may not furnish enough water for irrigation. From a chi standpoint, a deep river has stronger energy and is therefore more desirable than a shallow river.

Lastly, while ancient feng shui practitioners may not have worried about water pollution, modern-day practitioners do. Today, it is common to analyze a waterway's positive chi according to current, route, depth, and chemical levels.

SOIL

"Feng Shui is about looking at the soil and tasting the water," claimed ancient feng shui master Wu Zi Xu. Although this was said thousands of years ago, the sentiment still holds true today: Fertile soil with an abundance of nutrients, good drainage, and a balance of sunlight and moisture, is the ideal for most of the world's peoples. If the soil is not healthy, then an area will not be a healthy one to live in. The neolithic Chinese believed (and many modern Chinese still do) that regionally occurring illnesses were often directly related to poor soil: anemia from iron-scarce soil; goiters, thyroid conditions, and enlarged necks from iodine-deficient soil; and heart conditions from selenium-poor soil.

China's ancient peoples preferred soil that was delicate but not loose and moist but not wet. An area's flora and fauna helped early Chinese determine if soil was healthy. Before the advent of soil tests, they also tested soil by digging up a shovelful, sifting it, and gently dropping it—no tamping was allowed—back onto the spot from which it was taken. If the soil had risen slightly by the next morning, it signified that the soil had good chi. If the soil had dropped and become level with the dirt around it, it was said to have negative chi.

Healthy ground covering indicated fertile, chi-rich soil; it helped prevent erosion of precious soil; and, because plants are believed to attract energy, ground covering helped boost an area's overall chi.

GROUND COVERAGE

When studying the chi of a specific site, ancient feng shui masters considered the ground's coverage. Whether comprised of grass, shrubs, moss or other plants, the ideal ground covering was considered to be green and lush.

SITE CHECK: THINGS TO AVOID

The first thing a feng shui master does when analyzing an existing building or a building site is study the surrounding environment. When choosing a building site, it is generally wise to avoid a "poison arrow" location. Also known as "killing breath" or "shar", a poison arrow is negative chi which is said to carry misfortune, that can affect one's finances, career, family, health, romance, or overall luck. Poison arrows include anything directed at you in a straight line, such as a road, the pointed edges of buildings or objects, or even directly opposing doorways. Specific poison arrows to avoid include wind arrows, water arrows, earth arrows, stone arrows, and wood arrows.

WIND ARROWS

Because wind carries away good chi, it is considered unlucky to build a home in a windy location, such as on a mountain top or on a pier over a body of water.

WATER ARROWS

A fast-moving river, stream, or other body of water with an aggressive current can snatch chi and carry it away. Feng shui theory says that it is better to build near a moderately moving river or no river at all.

EARTH ARROWS

When feng shui masters talk about earth arrows, they are referring to inhospitable land with hard, depleted soil, no plant life, and an abundance of non-beneficial insects. This type of land fosters unhealthy chi, which the Chinese believe can lead to financial misfortune or poor health.

ROCK ARROWS

Generally speaking, sharp angles are avoided in feng shui. Sharp angles are believed to create negative influences that can hurt your body, which is why Chinese homes are rarely build on or around outcroppings of jagged rocks.

WOOD ARROWS

Because plants and trees are considered auspicious and conductors of strong beneficial chi, building a home in their midst is considered a good thing. However, an overabundance of trees or plants—such as a thick forest—creates a dense, sunless, stagnant environment that is also said to affect the normal flow of chi.

COMPASS SCHOOL (LI FA)

Early feng shui used the methods talked about in the Form School section (pages 24-29). It was not until well into the Sung dynasty (AD 960-1279) that feng shui scholars became interested in harmonizing an individual's energy with the energy from his or her surroundings. From these beliefs arose the Compass School, an ideology concerned with the best locations, directions, and situations for each individual.

Central to the Compass School are two mathematical squares developed by the early Chinese. The first of these patterns, the *he tu* or *ho t'u* (Yellow River) map was said to be given as a gift to the emperor Yu, founder of one of the Hsia dynasty (2000-1520 BC), one of China's most successful early dynasties. The ho t'u, as it is commonly known, was said to be a pattern of circles that marked the flank of a mythical dragon-horse who emerged from the Yellow River. While it is more probable that the ho t'u came from an ancient mathematician, its origins are unknown. What is known is that the diagram featured filled and unfilled circles—the filled circles representing yin and the unfilled circles representing yang. Each group of yin (even) circles is balanced on the opposite side of the diagram by an odd (yang) group of circles. Early philosophers believed that this complex pattern represented a fixed, ideal world in perfect harmony.

The second pattern integral to Compass School is the *l'o shu*, which was said to be carved into a turtle's shell that was subsequently found by Fu Hsi

L'O SHU

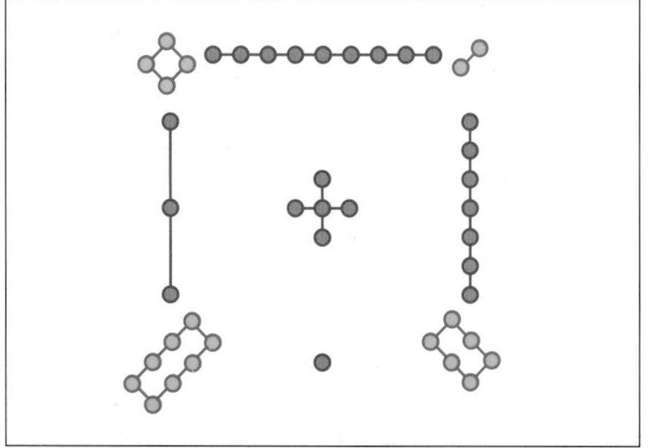

The blue "filled" evenly grouped circles symbolize yin; the orange "unfilled" oddly grouped circles are yang. Each row of circles—horizontal, vertical, or diagonal—adds up to 15.

HO T'U

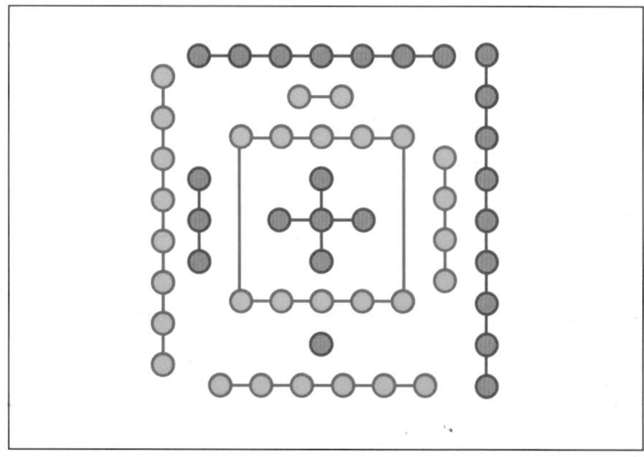

The outer and second layer of orange oddly grouped circles (1+3+7+9) and the outer and second layer of blue evenly grouped circles (1+3+7+9)—both add to 20.

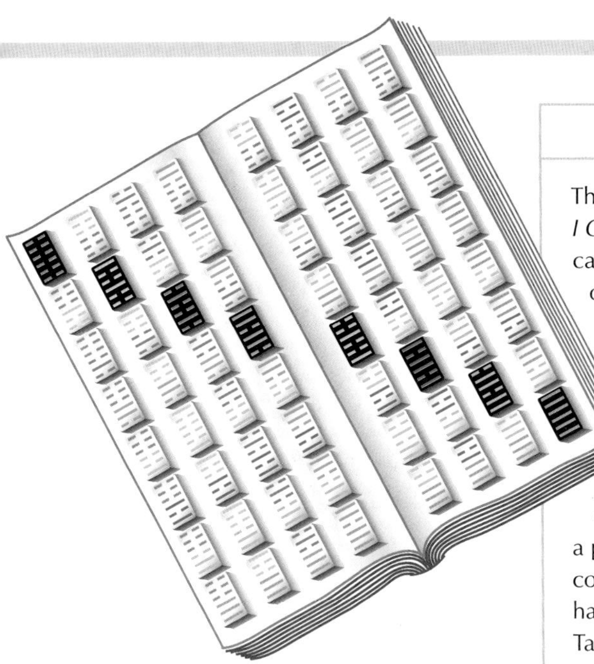

(or Wu of Hsia). Known also as the magic square of three, the pattern is believed to have been created by neolithic Chinese. Written in the ancient "Lo River language" of filled and unfilled circles, the diagram corresponds to the latter heaven sequence pa qua (see page 33). Each row of circles—whether horizontal, vertical, or diagonal—equals 15. The diagram is said to denote the interaction of natural and human chi. (Some scholars believe that the neolithic Chinese did use turtle shells to carve writings, thus giving the Chinese language its name of *chia gu*, or turtleback language.)

The Compass School is important in realms beyond feng shui. Its mathematical theories were adopted, adapted, and added to by Taoists of the time, making the two ideologies identical in regard to certain subject matters. Indeed, the *I Ching*, the pa qua, the five elements, and the Nine Palace—all discussed in the following pages—are as much a part of Taoism as they are feng shui.

THE BOOK OF CHANGES

There is much mystery surrounding the origins of the *I Ching*, which translates as "Book of Changes." Also called the *Yijing*, the *I Ching* is thought to be China's oldest book. Many scholars believe it was written over 6,000 years ago by Fu Hsi, China's first documented emperor (2953-2838 BC). Other experts believe the *I Ching* came about during the Han dynasty as a compilation of the *Zhouyi* (or the *Changes of Zhou*, an ancient text written during the Zhou dynasty) and subsequent books of Zhouyi commentary. Whatever its origins, the *I Ching* has had a profound effect on Chinese culture. Throughout the country's history, scholars, emperors, and military leaders have consulted it whenever a decision was to be made; Taoism (which is very closely associated with the *I Ching*) and Confucianism were built around the I Ching; and Chinese fortune tellers and feng shui experts continue to consult the book.

So what is the *I Ching* about? Changes, primarily. Without scientific knowledge, early civilizations had no way of knowing why earth, weather, stars, and other "natural" things behaved like they did. In explaining this, the book's author or authors came upon the theory of opposites, which later became known as yin and yang.

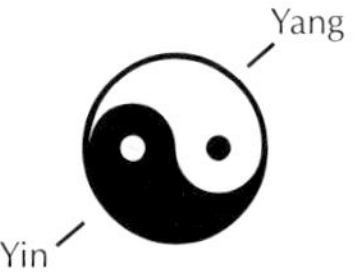

It was written that the interplay of opposites created energy—it was this energy (chi) that was responsible for not only creating the cosmos, but controlling what went on in the heavens and on earth. The *I Ching* also applied to humans, outlining an all-encompassing system for dissecting personality traits, fortune, health, romance, the future, and other human concerns. However, unlike Western books, the *I Ching* is not straight text. The book uses the symbols for Yin and Yang, as well as the trigrams (see p. 32) produced from them.

The *I Ching* documents three kinds of changes:

- **Constant**: The world is always and forever changing.
- **Simple**: The world changes according to simple rules.
- **None**: There is a way which a change will follow, and that way never changes.

PA KUA

To most Westerners, the *pa kua* (pronounced ba-gwar, and sometimes transliterated as *ba gua*) is a source of endless confusion. All those cryptic trigrams—many of which look so much alike! How possibly can a few black bars reveal the workings of the world, much less the future? Well, before getting to that, let's start with what the pa kua represents.

TRIGRAM	NAME	DIRECTION
☲	LI	S
☷	KUN	SW
☱	TUI	W
☰	CHIEN	NW
☵	KAN	N
☶	KEN	NE
☳	CHEN	E
☴	SUN	SE

The pa kua trigrams use two types of lines. One is a full line that represents yang, and the other is a broken line that represents yin. Every pa kua trigram is a combination of three of these types of lines. Within the pa kua, eight of these trigrams are used. Indeed, pa kua means eight (pa) trigrams (kua). Thus, English-speakers may prefer to think of the pa kua as eight ways of looking at life and the world.

The eight trigrams were devised by Fu Hsi, which he derived from a diagram that he found on the shell of a tortoise from the River Lo (see lo shu on pages 30–31). Fu Hsi went on to arrange the trigrams into an early pa kua known as the former heaven sequence (*hsien tien*). However, in about 1143 BC, the Duke of Wen, founder of the Chou Dynasty, created the arrangement used with the greatest frequency today. This popular arrangement is called the latter heaven sequence (*hu tien*).

But what does it all mean? Quite a few things, actually. Generally speaking, each trigram represents a transitional phase in nature or humans. Using the pa kua, you can determine your most auspicious—and inauspicious—directions and locations. Specifically speaking, each trigram represents a number of things, including a compass direction, a color, a body part, an illness, a number, a familial relation, an element, and more. Perhaps to make matters

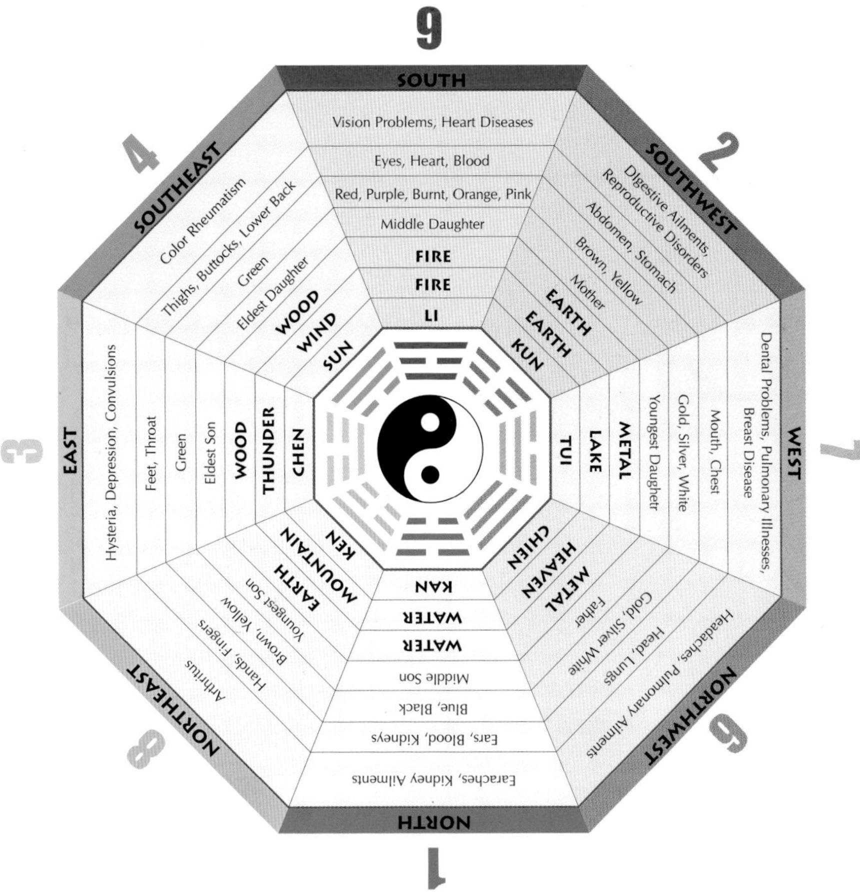

LATTER HEAVEN SEQUENCE PA KUA

This is the most popular pa kua used today. Note that at the turn of the 20th century, some Chinese feng shui masters adopted the Western custom of orienting north at the top (the above pa kua is more traditional in that the south is on top). Whether north or south is on the top, the orientation does not affect how the pa kua is used.

more confusing, these trigrams are arranged in an octagon—often with a yin and yang symbol or a compass in the middle. Following Chinese custom, the trigram indicating south is always at the top, and the north trigram at the bottom, east trigram to the left, and west trigram to the right.

DIRECTION FINDER

The Chinese's awareness of the earth magnetic field dates back to the Shang Dynasty (1650–1027 BC). However, it was not until 500 BC during the Zhou Dysnasty that this information was used as an orientation aid. At that time, orientation instruments were created in such shapes as needles, spoons, and disks; these were used to establish magnetic and geographic constants. Eventually, the four directions, the five elements, the pa kua, the four seasons, Chinese astrology charts, and more were engraved on the base of the Chinese compass, which was fashioned with over 24 rings or "layers." These layers provided easy access to information that feng shui masters needed for their work.

THE EIGHT TRIGRAMS

The eight trigrams of the pa kua are more than pretty designs, they each represent something specific. The symbols are read from the bottom line up: The bottom line represents earth, the middle line represents mankind and the top line represents heaven. The lower row of these figures determines whether the overall symbol is yin (broken line) or yang (straight line).

Chien (Qian, The Creative, Father)

Symbol: Heaven
Element: Metal
Color: Gold, silver, white
Body Part: Head, lungs
Illness: Headaches, pulmonary ailments
Number :6
Chien consists of three yang (unbroken lines). It represents strong, persistent energy (chi). Located in the northwest position, it symbolizes the father or husband—or a business's president or country's ruler—and the rooms he would most likely use, such as the study, den, or office. The season Chien represents is the time between late fall and early winter.

Kun (Kun, The Receptive, Mother)

Symbol: Earth
Element: Earth
Color: Brown, yellow
Body Part: Abdomen, stomach
Illness: Digestive ailments, reproductive disorders
Number: 2
Kun is comprised of three yin (broken) lines. It represents nurturing, receptive chi. Located in the southwest, Kun symbolizes the mother and the rooms that were once associated with mothers, including the kitchen and dining room. The season Kun represents is late summer.

Chen (Zhen, The Arousing, Eldest Son)

Symbol: Thunder
Element: Wood
Color: Green
Body Part: Feet, throat
Illness: Hysteria, depression, convulsions
Number: 3
Chen is made up of one yang (unbroken) line and two yin (broken) lines. It represents decisiveness, suddenness, and unexpected energy. Located in the east, Chen symbolizes the eldest son, suggesting his bedroom should be in the east. The season Chen represents is early spring.

Sun (Xun, The Gentle, Eldest Daughter)

Symbol: Wind
Element: Wood
Color: Green
Body Part: Thighs, buttocks, lower back
Illness: Colds, rheumatism
Number: 4
Sun is built of one yin (broken) line beneath two yang (unbroken) lines. It represents wholeness, a good and sound mind, and great inner strength. Located in the southeast, Sun symbolizes the eldest daughter; her bedroom should be in the southeast part of the house. Sun represents late spring or early summer.

THE EIGHT TRIGRAMS

Kan (The Abysmal, Middle Son)

Symbol: Water
Element: Water
Color: Blue, black
Body Part: Ears, blood, kidneys
Illness: Earaches, kidney ailments
Number: 1
Kan is fashioned from two yin (broken) lines on either side of a yang (unbroken) line. It represents ambitious, driven, industrious (though sometimes deceitful) chi. Located in the north, Kan symbolizes the middle brother, suggesting his bedroom should sit in the northern part of the house. The season Kan represents is winter.

Li (Li, The Clinging, Middle Daughter)

Symbol: Fire
Element: Fire
Color: Red, purple, burnt orange, pink
Body Part: Eyes, heart, blood
Illness: Vision problems, heart diseases
Number: 9
Li is formed from one yin (broken line) between two yang (unbroken) lines. It represents successful, brilliant, warm chi. Located in the south, Li symbolizes the middle daughter, meaning the southern part of the house would be the best place for her bedroom. The season Li represents is summer.

Ken (Gen, Keeping Still, Youngest Son)

Symbol: Mountain
Element: Earth
Color: Brown, yellow
Body Part: Hands, fingers
Illness: Arthritis
Number: 8
Ken consists of a yang (unbroken) line atop two yin (broken) lines. It represents solid, stable, intuitive chi. Located in the northeast, Ken symbolizes the youngest son, making the northeast part of the home the best place for his bedroom. The season Ken represents is late winter.

Tui (Dui The Joyful, Youngest Daughter)

Symbol: Lame
Element: Metal
Color: Gold, silver, white
Body Part: Mouth, chest
Illness: Dental problems, pulmonary illnesses, breast diseases
Number: 7
Tui is composed of a yin (broken) line atop two yang (unbroken) lines. It represents happy, satisfied chi. Located in the west, Tui symbolizes the youngest daughter, meaning the western part of the house is ideal for her bedroom. The season Tui represents is autumn.

FIVE ELEMENTS

The Compass School utilizes a tenet of Chinese philosophy called the "five elements" or "five phases of Chinese astrology."The five elements are fire, earth, metal, water, and wood, each with their own distinct energy that either harmonizes or opposes other elements.

The element theory was inspired by China's varied topography and climates. Early Chinese civilization, which started in central China, looked at its own region and saw a neutral climate with yellow soil; the north was cold with black soil; the south was hot with red soil; the east had warm weather and gray-green soil; and the west was cool and dry with white soil. To correspond with the temperatures and soil types, the ancient Chinese assigned each of these regions an element category: central China was symbolized by earth, northern China was represented by water, southern China was symbolized by fire, eastern China was represented by wood, and western China was represented by metal. By the time of the Han dynasty (207 BC–AD 220) planets, tastes, seasons, sounds, internal organs, shapes, birth order, numbers, and other items were added until each of the five elements categories represented a group of concepts. Even human birthdays are relegated to five element categories. To find out which category you belong to, turn to the "Chinese Calendar" on page 173.

To the uninitiated, the five elements look like a simple roundup of natural elements. But it is more than that. To the Chinese, the five elements (including all the items within each element) represent the movements of chi. Here is how it works: Each element has its own chi character and thus interacts with other elements in specific ways. Fire chi ascends, earth chi revolves, metal chi tightens, water chi flows downward, and wood chi enlarges. It is the way that the five elements interact with one other that decides the balance of chi in nature, buildings, and even within ourselves.

The Chinese believe that fire, earth, metal, water, and wood are the five key elements that affect our daily lives on Earth.

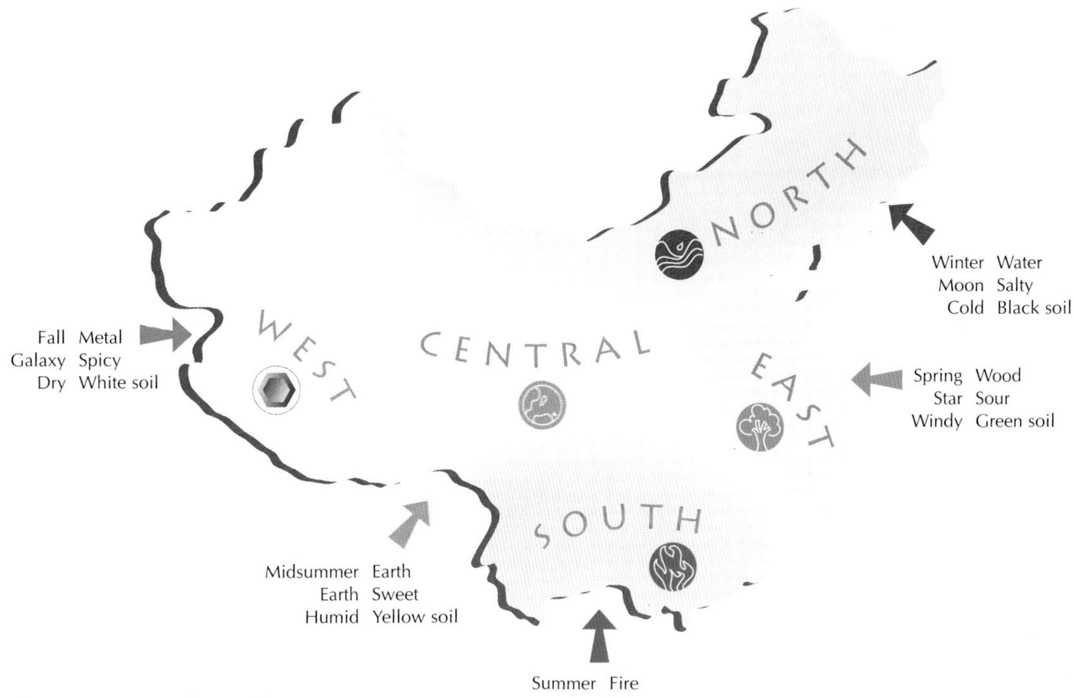

China and Five Elements

The origins of the five element theory go back to ancient China, when each region of the country was assigned an element based on its climate and soil type.

ELEMENTAL CYCLES

Within the five elements there are cycles called the productive cycle, the domination cycle, and the reductive cycle. The productive cycle, known also as the birth cycle, is a positive, productive cycle in which each of the elements—fire, earth, metal, water, and wood—helps create the element that follows it. Thus fire produces, or gives birth to, earth chi. Earth spins around itself to produces the contractive chi of metal. Metal contracts into liquid, symbolizing water chi. Water nourishes the growth of wood chi, and wood gives fuel so that fire chi might burn. The balanced progression of the productive cycle represents harmony and creation.

The domination cycle is a chaotic cycle of imbalance which weakens and even depletes chi. Sometimes referred to as the destructive

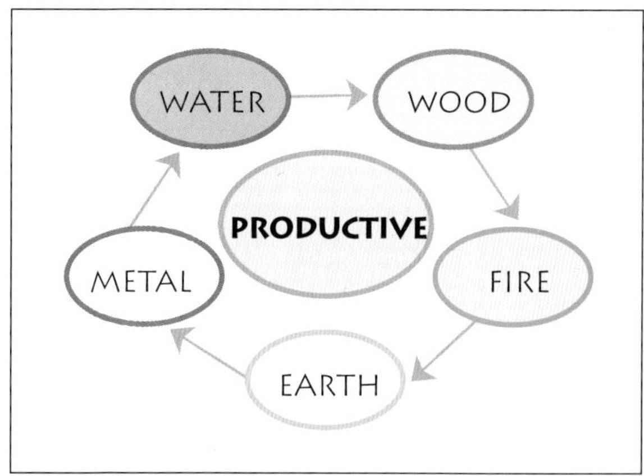

The productive cycle is often called the birth cycle because each element helps give birth to the one next in order.

cycle, the Chinese believe that it causes environmental imbalances (such as Global Warming) and human illnesses (such as weakened immune systems). Within the domination cycle, each element overpowers the element sitting two places away from it; thus fire melts metal, earth dams waterflow, metal pierces wood, water douses fire, and wood scars or depletes earth.

The reductive cycle is a healing cycle used to remedy the imbalance created by the domination cycle; each element reduces the strength of the element that precedes it. Fire burns wood, wood absorbs water, water corrodes metal, metal moves the earth, and earth reduces fire. This cycle can be practically applied to life situations: a person who feels they have an excess of the water element can find balance by adding wood to their environment.

WATER
WOOD
METAL
FIRE
EARTH

DOMINATION CYCLE

In the domination or destructive cycle, each element overpowers the one that follows it.

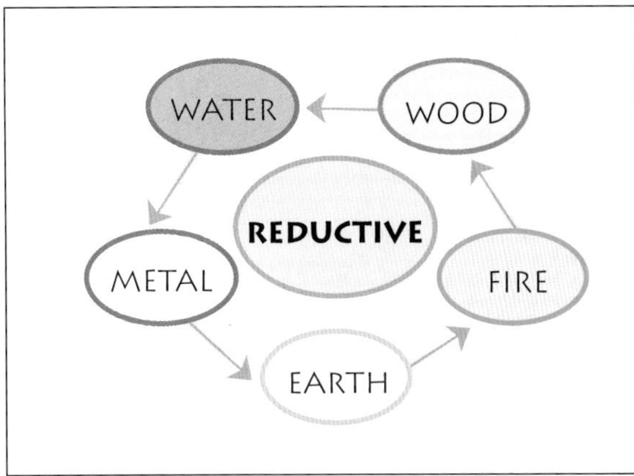

The reductive or controlling cycle is used to create balance by restoring the five element's productive sequence of chi.

NINE PALACES

The Nine Palaces go by many names. Known also as the Nine Floating Stars, the Flying Stars, the Purple-White Flying Palace, the Purple-White Flying Stars, and the Purple-White Nine Stars, the Nine Palaces are the seven stars of the big dipper constellation, plus two invisible companion stars. Early in China's history, these nine stars were believed to make up the throne of emperors of the Shang dynasty (c. 1650–1027 BC). During the Western Chin dynasty (AD 265–316), the Nine Palaces were considered actual gods; in the Tang (AD 618–906) dynasty, the Nine Palaces represented nine archtypical, chi-balanced mountains where spirit gods lived. It was during the recent Ching dynasty (1644-1912), that the term "Nine Palaces" came to be applied to a feng shui system that studied auspicious and inauspicious times during any given period for both humans and buildings.

For many people, the Nine Palaces is the most confusing system within feng shui. Although we will not be focusing it in this book, it is important to understand the basic concept. The Nine Palaces use the numbered lo shu magic squares (see page 30), assigning each number a meaning that is then used to predict future events. While there is a universal Nine Palaces chart (also known as a universal luo shu chart or table) that is used for general feng shui questions, for an extremely accurate feng shui reading, the Nine Palaces chart must be rotated to correspond to specific 20-year periods the earth is in. This is where things get confusing. Currently, the earth is in the seventh period, which encompasses the years from 1984 to 2003 (the eighth period begins in 2004 and ends in 2025). What does this mean? The universal Nine Palaces chart's central number changes into a 7 at the beginning of the period

THE UNIVERSAL NINE PALACES

4 **southeast** wood love, sex, education	9 **south** fire good luck, future prosperity	2 **south west** earth ill health
3 **east** wood anger, stress, disputes	5 **yellow** earth oppression, misfortune	7 **west** metal communication, entertainment, spiritual matters
8 **north east** earth very good fortune, prosperity in near future	1 **north** water overall good fortune	6 **north west** metal prosperity

1984–2003. The universal central number happens to always be a 5, so all that is necessary at the beginning of this period is adding a 2. But, you cannot simply add 2 only to the center position—each number gets two extra numbers added to it! However, because only single digit numbers are allowed on the chart, the universal chart's 8 becomes a 10 (8+2=10, which is reduced further by adding the 1 and 0 to get 1). The universal chart's nine becomes an 11, which, when broken down to a single digit of two.

IT'S ALL RELATED

All of the symbols and formulas used within the Compass School are related. Some of them were born of the same theory, and others were created to complement an existing concept. For instance, it is believed that the Nine Palaces theory was developed in response to the ho t'u and lo shu squares. In homage to the Nine Palaces, Fu Hsi perfected the pa qua. Later the Yellow Emperor developed the five elements using the concepts of the pa qua. And all of these sub-theories are indebted to the concept of yin and yang.

Big Dipper Constellation

The Nine Palaces theory partly refers to the seven stars of the Big Dipper, plus two invisible companion stars.

Lo Shu

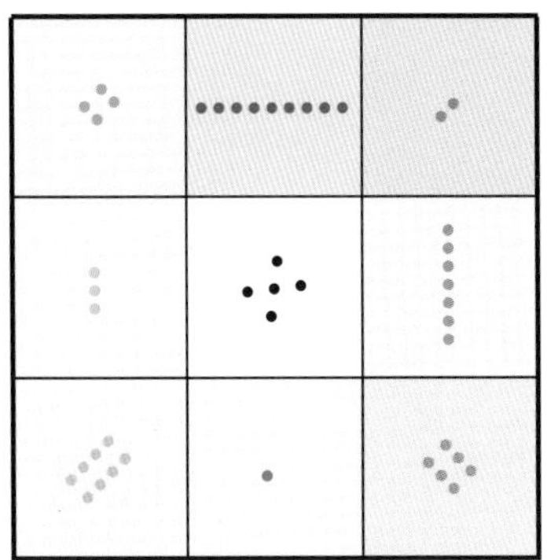

In this lo shu chart, the even groups of numbers are yin and the odd yang.

Nine Palaces

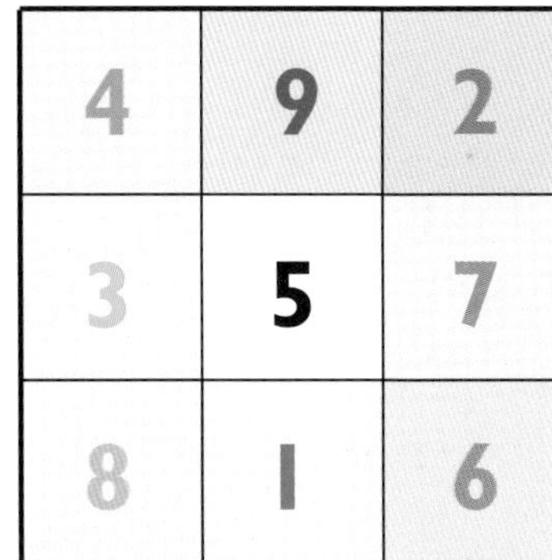

The number sets from the lo shu chart were adapted into the nine palaces.

Pa Qua

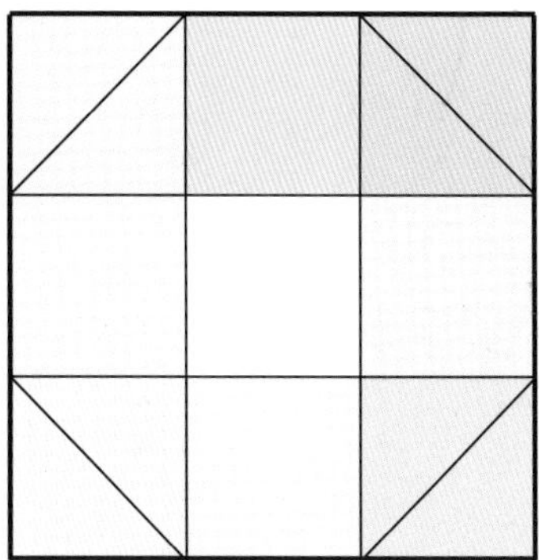

The pa qua was derived from the Nine Palaces theory, and added trigrams.

DEFINING YIN AND YANG

On page 8 we talked a little bit about yin and yang (see "Yin, Yang, and Chi"), the Chinese concept denoting the two opposing forces that exist within every living thing. Within feng shui theory, yin and yang holds a special place. There is yin and yang in nature, in building sites, in buildings, and also in individual rooms.

Yin and yang are not fixed concepts, but relative ones. In other words, an object is pronounced yin or yang in the context of its environment. For instance, a mountain is generally considered a yang object, yet when it is behind a house, it is yin and the house is yang. Although this sounds confusing, it is actually quite simple: When two objects are near each other, whichever has the most active energy is yang, and whichever has the most receptive energy is yin.

For example, let's take one room and dress it in two different ways: When painted a dark color, kept at a cool temperature, and rarely entered, the room is said to be too yin. When painted a light color, kept at a warm temperature, and crowded with people, plants, and/or pets, the room is said to be too yang.

Use blinds or shades to balance an overly sunny (yang) room.

Topic	Yin	Yang
mountain	side facing away from the sun	side facing the sun
house	back face	front face
house and mountain	mountain	house
mountain and water	water	mountain
wall and interior	wall	inside space
city wall and city	city wall	city
skin and blood circulation	skin	blood circulation

A balanced room is defined by a number of yin and yang factors, but comfort is also important.

Balancing the feng shui in rooms requires certain adjustments. The yin room will achieve a more balanced energy when yang elements are added. This can be done by painting the room a lighter color, raising the temperature a few degrees, or allowing people and pets to use the room more often. In the yang room, balance may be achieved by drawing the curtain either fully or partially to keep out bright sun, lowering the temperature a few degrees, or installing a calming water fountain. These are all ways to raise the yin energy and lower the yang energy until the two are balanced.

PART TWO

FENG SHUI AT HOME

CHAPTER THREE

BASIC FENG SHUI FOR ANY LIVING SPACE

WHETHER YOU LIVE IN A CITY APARTMENT OR A COUNTRY HOUSE, HERE ARE THE FUNDAMENTAL FENG SHUI GUIDELINES FOR CREATING POSITIVE ENERGY IN YOUR HOME

THE KEY 3

When Americans think about feng shui, chances are they think of something that can better the look and feel of their living spaces. Called residential feng shui, its purpose is to enhance the flow of healthy chi throughout a house or apartment, which in turn can improve the health, wealth, family relations, career, and luck of a home's residents.

As mentioned in Chapter 2, there are two main schools of feng shui: Form School and the Compass School. Within residential feng shui there are practitioners that use one school or the other, and a

Front doors are "gates" that can help attract auspicious energy into your home, while keeping inauspicious chi out.

Today we have many other sources for food, yet kitchens are still the central cooking and gathering spaces in our homes.

Good sleep is crucial for maintaining good health and relieving stress, so a well-planned bedroom is important.

number of experts that use both schools simultaneously. However, because this book concentrates on feng shui for beginners, the Form School is its primary focus. However, it is interesting to look at the whole process. When analyzing a home, a Compass School practitioner generally consults the Chinese astrological charts for a home's residents, calculating their personal trigrams, and from that whether they are a member of the east or west house group (see page 179). Next, a Flying Star or universal nine palaces chart is created, then rotated according to the year the house was built. A plan of the house or apartment is drawn up and the palaces are superimposed on this diagram. The home is then rearranged according to all the above factors.

Before getting started, it should be mentioned that traditionally, the key three areas in residential design are the front door, the bedroom, and the kitchen; early feng shui concentrated most heavily on these three elements. In ancient China, the front door was believed to keep out evil spirits, thus the style, color, and shape of door became important factors that could help protect a home's residents. With the early Chinese emphasis on descendents—and because one-third of a person's life is spent sleeping—it was crucial that the bedchamber was a room of healthy, propitious chi. This is why ancient feng shui practitioners spent so much effort on the ideal layout of this room. In days when food was not as accessible as it is today, the kitchen literally was a source of life support. In ancient feng shui, it was important to situate the kitchen to please what is generally referred to as the "kitchen god." Later, a kitchen's layout served to make this important, and sometimes dangerous room—with its knives, fire, and sometimes slippery floors—safe and efficient.

As homes and lifestyles change, feng shui faces the challenge of adapting to new rooms (separate family and living rooms did not exist in ancient China, nor were there fitness or other specialty rooms); new living spaces (apartments had not been invented when feng shui began); plumbing; new types of furniture (including electronic devices), non-Chinese cultural styles and customs, and many other different ways of living.

DOORS

THE FRONT DOOR AND ENTRYWAY

A house's or apartment's front door is a barrier that separates outdoor energy from indoor energy. More specifically, this door contains a home's auspicious interior chi while protecting occupants from any inauspicious chi that may be lurking outside. Because the Chinese consider the front entrance the most important door in a home (and the most practical from a protective standpoint), it should be larger and stronger than the interior doors. However, the front door should be in proportion to the rest of the home. For example, a large door can encourage propitious chi to leak from a small house, leading to financial hardship. Likewise, a small door can make it hard for chi to enter a large home, making the occupants feel stifled and argumentative.

Furthermore, consideration should be given to what the front door opens to reveal. Because it is the first thing a person sees, the entryway or foyer represents a home—meaning those that pass through it are affected by the chi it contains. To attract beneficial chi, an entry should be as airy as possible, uncluttered, attractive, with plenty of

Door 2

Door 1

The entrance door to your home is more important than any interior door. The entrance door should ideally be bigger than the interior doors.

A stairway leading straight from the front door directly to the second floor is believed by some feng shui practitioners to be neutral. Others believe that this situation encourages chi from the entrance to race up the stairs too rapidly into the home.

A split staircase near the entrance—with one flight connecting the lower and ground level, and another flight connecting the ground and second floors—is slightly less harmful than a single straight stairway connecting the ground and lower levels. The remedy used in the example to the right is appropriate here.

In a house, it is inauspicious if stairs near the front door lead directly to and from a lower level. To keep beneficial chi from racing down the stairs into the cellar, a feng shui adjustment must be made. Installing a door at the top of the basement stairs redirects the good chi through the rest of the house.

light (either natural or artificial). A strong front door is of little use if it opens to reveal a dark, dank, dirty, or cluttered entryway. An unkempt entry attracts and stores negative chi, meaning when the front door opens, negative chi will rush into the foyer and stay there long after the door has been shut.

Many western-style homes feature a stairway off the entry, and apartment doors often face stairways. From a feng shui standpoint, a front door and a stairway facing each other can be less than ideal if the stairway leads to a lower floor, such a recreation room or basement. In the case of a house, it is believed that a home's auspicious chi will speed down the stairs once the front door is opened, instead of benefiting the occupants. The best remedy is to reposition the stairway. If this is impossible, the situation can be corrected by installing a door at the top of the stairway.

Basement apartment dwellers have a slightly different problem. If their front door faces a descending stairway that leads from the apartment building entrance, they will receive overly harsh chi. A small mirror hung above the outside of the front door offers some protection.

SHAR

The Chinese believe that all mass contains energy. More specifically, they believe that sharp angles contain negative energy. Thus, any angle pointing at a front door or any of a home's interior doors, will impose its energy both on the door and the room behind the door. Known as a *shar* or "poison arrow," these angles can consist of a corner of the building across the street, a place where two interior walls meet, a piece of art, a free-standing screen, a rectangular column, or even a tree trunk, among other things.

Because of the way western houses are designed, most homes contain at least a few shars, most commonly where walls meet each other. Keep in mind the relative size of the shar and the door which the shar is pointing towards. A big, thick door will be less effected by a small shar—say the corner of a sculpture—than will a thin interior door. Still, if you can remedy a shar, most feng shui masters would suggest doing so.

PROBLEMS

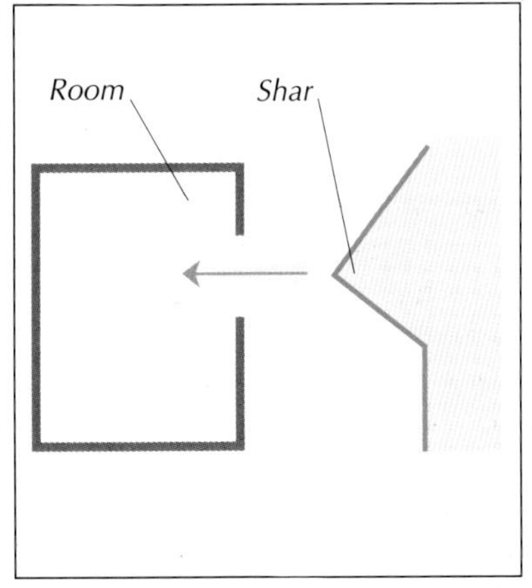

Sharp angles (shars) that point directly at front doors—either from walls, edges of elevators, or other objects—are common in apartment buildings.

A shar can generate strong negative energy for the room it points at, however, the smaller the size of the shar, the less energy it generates.

A building's corner shar is not as destructive when it is split in two. The bottom of this edifice is less harmful than the top.

SOLUTIONS

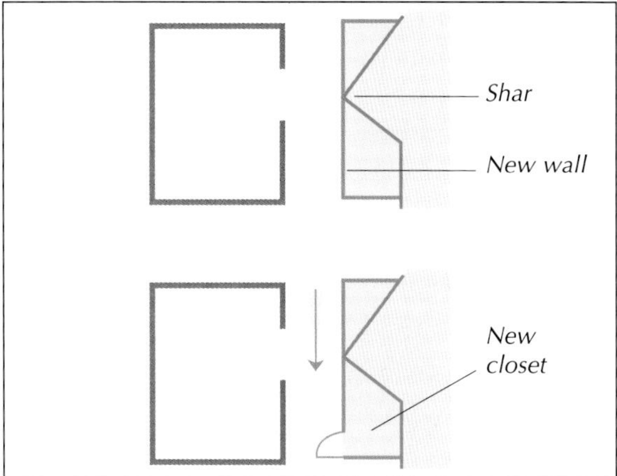

You can block a shar's energy by eliminating or filling in the angle; one way is to build a new wall (top) or closet (bottom).

Apartment interiors gain protection from outdoor shars with well-arranged elevator areas that act as buffers.

If you cannot build a wall to block an interior shar, a large houseplant or potted tree can soften the offending angle.

STAIRWAYS AND ELEVATORS

Stairways and elevators are the arteries of a building, whether in an apartment building or a house. Compared with a building's horizontal pull of hallways, stairways and elevators draw chi in a vertical direction. In general, the vertical energy flow is slower and more leisurely than horizontal energy flow. While they are often seen as positive elements within a building, stairways can be negative if they both face the front door and connect a lower floor. As for elevators, because they are noisy and move in a stop-and-start fashion, many feng shui practitioners believe they can affect the smooth flow of chi into apartments that are next to or across from them.

DOOR PLACEMENT

It is common in western-style homes to have a hallway or room with doors that directly face each other. In feng shui, this is considered inauspicious, creating antagonistic, claustrophobic, and frustrated energy. When two or more doors are placed on what feng shui practitioners call "one line," the energy speeds too quickly from door to door and immediately departs, leaving no health, wealth, or other auspicious benefits. Adjusting the doors in such a situation is difficult and can leave some rooms hard to access by a home's occupants, so to encourage chi to linger a while longer, other types of feng shui adjustments must be made to slow down the energy's pace. The easiest of these is to alternate floor-bound and ceiling-bound objects near the doors to pull chi in a more gentle, undulating pattern. Of course you do not want to clutter your doorways, but a large, lush plant placed near one door and a wind chime hung near the next door can encourage the energy to take a more leisurely pace.

PROBLEM

A corridor or room with two facing doors encourages chi to hurry through a home, leaving occupants untouched by its many benefits.

SOLUTION

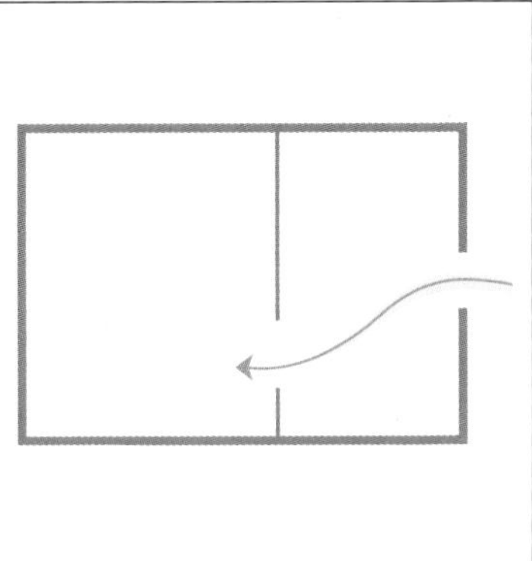

Move one of the doors so that the chi is forced to move through the home in a more leisurely manner..

Screens, fish tanks, and wind chimes are some of the objects that can be used for redirecting and slowing down energy between facing doors.

MIRRORS

Mirrors play an interesting role within feng shui. Because they were not part of early Chinese homes, feng shui theory has had to adapt to make room for these common household items. Many feng shui practitioners (especially those who belong exclusively to the Compass School) do not recognize mirrors as a legitimate feng shui remedy. Other practitioners believe that mirrors are powerful tools that can be used to reflect energy. Be aware that chi-reflecting is not always a good thing. For instance, a mirror placed facing an interior door will reflect the energy back into the room. This is a very harsh situation and should be avoided. If the mirror can not be moved, cover it with a curtain or some other decoration to reduce energy loss.

PROBLEM

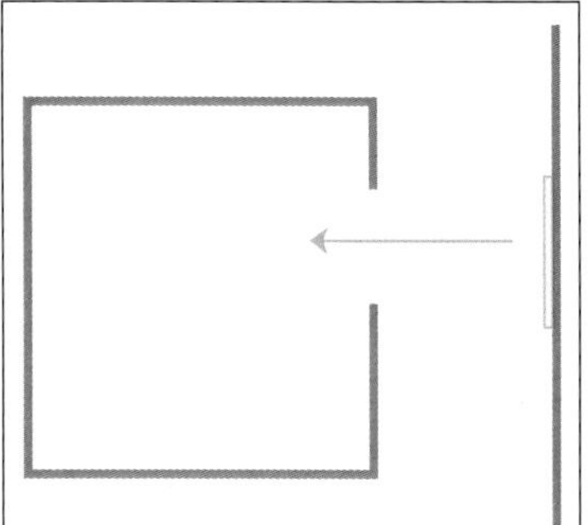

A mirror facing a door reflects inauspicious chi back into the room. Note, however, that the smaller the mirror, the less chi it will reflect.

SOLUTION

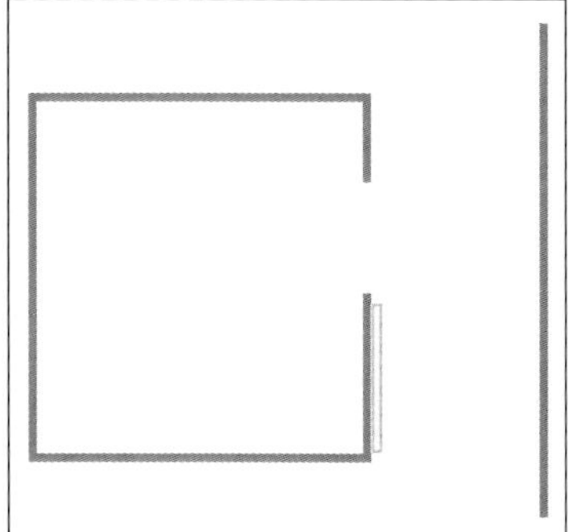

Move the mirror to another location or change it to a painting.

Although you should not hang a mirror so that it faces a room's door, placing it in an area where it faces into the room—as in the above example—can help increase yang energy in a room that is too yin.

BEDROOMS

Since humans do spend one-third of their lives sleeping, the Chinese—who believe good-quality sleep is one of the most important factors in good health—spend a great deal of energy designing their bedrooms.

Good air circulation, daytime light, and soft, calming, colors are essential to a good flow of chi within the bedroom. Using the space under your bed for storage, stashing things behind the door, leaving yesterday's clothes strewn about the floor, or having a disorderly closet are believed to trap negative energy within a room, which can interfere with quality sleep, as well as affect one's health, career, relationships, and overall luck. Indeed, one of the easiest ways to boost the bedroom's—or any room's—auspicious chi is to get rid of the clutter.

BEDS AND DOORS

When analyzing a bedroom, one of the first things a feng shui master will note is the position of the bed in relation to the door. In feng shui theory, it is important for you to be able to see from your bed anyone who might come through the bedroom door. Also, it is believed that if the door opens onto or behind the head of the bed, the strong energy from the door can make you ill. Other inauspicious positions include "the death" position (said by the Chinese to suggest the position of a coffin before it leaves a home for the mortuary), in which the foot of the bed directly faces the door.

A Compass School master may also suggest positioning your bed so that your head will be in that particular year's wealth corner or in your most auspicious direction to attract auspicious chi. If you would like to try this yourself, use a compass and the information on pages 30-37.

However, most modern bedrooms do not offer the space or flexibility to be able to reposition the bed

If the door opens directly onto the head of the bed, the energy entering the room will hit the head of the person sleeping there, causing headaches and illness.

The best position for a bed is diagonally facing the door; this layout provides safe harbor for the bed's occupants.

regularly according to one's charts. That is why the Form School works to enhance auspicious chi within the constraints of one's environment. From a Form School standpoint, the most beneficial place to place a bed is usually as near as possible to the corner diagonally opposite the door. This does not always hold true, however, as we shall see later—as there are also walls, windows, and kitchen positions to consider.

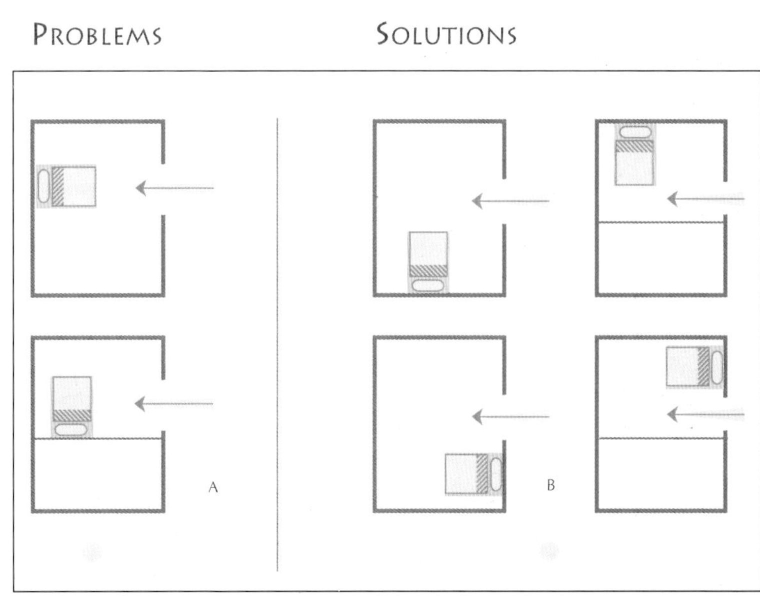

Both floor plans in diagram A depict inauspicious bed/door layouts. The solutions in the top row of diragram B are more protective than those in the lower row.

WALLS, WINDOWS, AND BEDS

A bed placed in the middle of a room can make a sleeper feel unsettled and unstable. That's why in feng shui, beds are placed preferably with the headboard against a wall. This provides the sleeper with strong and secure chi.

It is pure common sense: A bed should be located in an area that is quiet, safe and draft-free. That is why most feng shui practitioners also advise against placing a bed under or in close proximity to a window. Even with the window closed, there is often still a draft. In fact, in China, it is believed that cool drafts from a window contribute to headaches in healthy individuals and Bell's palsy in elderly or weak individuals.

The distance between the headboard and the window is key, and should be determined by factoring the force of the window draft, the direction of the window, the height of the bed, whether a heater or air conditioner sits by the window, or if there are any curtains on the window or around the bed (see the box on the next page fors distance guidelines).

A bed placed in the middle of the room is said in feng shui to be "floating," creating an atmosphere of instability and anxiousness in the bedroom.

While it is preferable to anchor a bed to the wall by its headboard, if needed, a bed can be situated with one of its sides against a wall. Although this is not as favored as the first example, having a side against a wall can help create a feeling of safety.

Unfortunately, many modern bedrooms are designed in such a way that the door and closets occupy one wall, with windows on the wall opposite, not leaving many bed-placement options for a person. In instances where a bed must be placed against or near a window, many feng shui masters recommend counteracting the window's effects by placing a full, heavy canopied curtain around the bed. At one time, these types of curtains were common in China and can still be found in some home design and furniture stores.

The bed shown here is situated at an appropriate distance from the windows, whether they are facing southeast or northwest.

It is a common belief in China that if you sleep near a window you can develop headaches, or in severe cases, Bell's palsy.

WINDOW AND BED SITING

For individuals who cannot avoid placing a bed near a window, the following guide offers some help on just how far away a bed should be from a window.

- A window facing southeast: 3 feet
- A window facing northwest: 6 feet
- A tall bed which has a mattress that sits higher than the window-sill: 3 feet higher than the sill
- A bed that is on the floor: 6 feet
- A window with a heater below it: 3 feet
- A window with an air conditioning unit under it: 6 feet
- A bed with a full canopied curtain: 3 feet
- A bed with no canopied curtain: 6 feet

HEADBOARDS AND DRESSERS

For individuals wishing to fine-tune their bedroom's chi, it is possible to choose a bed's headboard to complement one's element. The shape of the headboard can be designed to be in accord with the owner's elements which are determined by the person's birthday. To determine your element, turn to pages 172–173.

HEADBOARD SHAPES BY ELEMENT

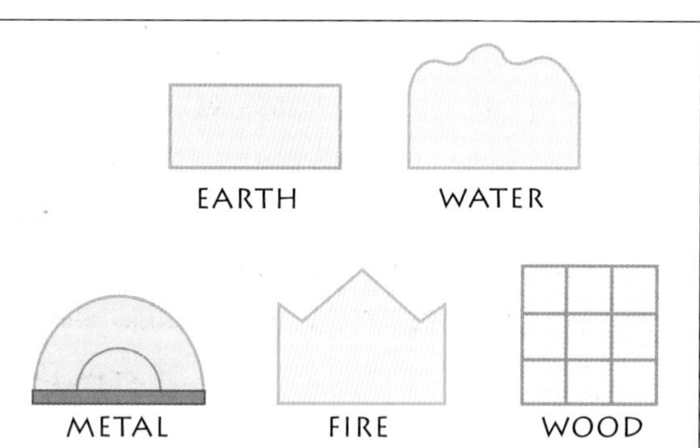

If a bed is to be shared by two people of different elements, they can choose an option that will best complement both elements (for more information, see pages 172–173). The objective is to avoid choosing a headboard shape representing an element that might clash with their own element.

Dressers are the second most common type of bedroom furniture, after the bed. Here, we have expanded the term to include traditional dressers, chests of drawers, and armoires. These should not be placed right next to the head of a bed—doing so is said to disrupt the room's chi, making it difficult for energy to pass over anyone who happens to be in the bed. Neither should the corner of a dresser point directly at the bed. Such a corner generates a shar and is believed to foster negative energy.

Good chi will not reach the people sleeping in the above bed, as the dresser is too close to (and taller than) the mattress.

For a metal person, this headboard is the ideal shape and material; however, the night table should be moved away from the bed to allow the chi to flow more freely.

BEAMS AND STAIRWAYS

Many European-style homes feature heavy, exposed beams, a much-sought after design element in western culture. In China, however, exposed beams—especially in the bedroom—are believed to attract negative feng shui by creating the sensation of great weight. This constricts positive chi and can affect family harmony and finances. If a drop ceiling cannot be installed to conceal a beam, some feng shui experts recommend covering it with fabric.

Whatever you do to remedy an exposed beam, there is one thing you must be mindful of: Never sleep under a beam or with any other objects (such as a windchime or ceiling light) directly over your head. The Chinese believe this distracts a person, causing restless sleep. To see how you are affected by having something hanging over your head, try lying down facing the ceiling. Get a friend to hold their hand over your face, pointing their index finger down toward the space between your eyes. You will likely find this annoying at best, very unsettling at worst.

Exposed ceiling beams create negative energy in a bedroom. It is best to cover them with a drop ceiling or fabric.

When it comes to bed placement, stairways are treated much like beams or other heavy objects hanging over one's head. Although it is not common to have a room situated under a stairway, it does occur in small attic rooms, A-frame cabins, and in homes where a small room has been fashioned under a stairway. In all of these situations, the bed should be situated so it is not directly under the stairway.

Overhanging stairs create a sense of pressure and weight; this constricts positive chi and can affect family harmony and finances. From a practical standpoint, sleeping under a staircase can cause broken sleep; when people climb or descend the stairs, the vibration will disturb the sleeper. These vibrations can also affect air quality by loosening ceiling dust and paint chips, which may fall on the sleeper below.

Beds should not be placed under stairways. The stairs create a subconcious feeling of overhead pressure that impairs sleep.

BEDROOM MIRRORS

In western bedrooms, mirrors are common. Most dressers and vanities come with matching mirrors, and there is usually a full-length mirror on the back of a door or somewhere else in the room so one can check their "look" before leaving the house. The use of mirrors is debatable: while not all feng shui experts believe mirrors are powerful, many practitioners see them as inauspicious. Some experts feel they are acceptable in children's rooms, but all agree that they should be avoided in couple's rooms. Mirrors are said to reflect aggressive energy into the bedroom and strain the relationship of the couple who sleeps there; they can also cause bad relationship luck to the single person. A mirror that faces a bed is particularly unsettling; as a rule of thumb, you should not be able to see your reflection while in bed.

Luckily, you do not have to give up all of your mirrors. Simply place full-length mirrors on the inside of closet doors (which can be shut when not needed) and limit other mirrors to small-sized versions. In feng shui, an object's power is relative to its size; thus a small mirror has less negative power than a large mirror. Couples who like to use mirrors during lovemaking are encouraged to either use a separate "play bedroom" for this purpose, or to cover the mirrors with curtains or fabric when not in use.

Never place a big mirror facing the bed. Its agressive energy is said to affect one's well-being and damage love relationships.

A dresser with a mirror should not face the bed. If you have a dresser with an attached mirror that you would like to keep in your bedroom, consider placing it in a direction facing away from the bed.

CLOCKS AND ELECTRONIC DEVICES

Thousands of years ago when feng shui was first developed, there was no electricity, which meant no clocks, computers, fax machines, radios, stereos, television sets, or any of the other electronic paraphernalia often found in modern day bedrooms. Feng shui's view on such items is this: if possible, do not put them in the bedroom, if that is impossible, then do not put them anywhere near the bed. Why? Because feng shui practitioners—along with some modern-day scientists—know that these electrical items create electromagnetic fields which are believed to contribute to headaches, irregular heart beats, and shallow respiration (see pages 158–159 for further information.) Feng shui practitioners also believe that this electromagnetic field impairs the quality of sleep and can lead to insomnia by disrupting the REM (rapid eye movement) sleep phase.

Electronic devices such as computers and TVs are best kept out of the bedroom, or a good distance from the bed. Their strong electromagnetic waves can impair sleep.

Clocks are best put in the study, office, or other part of the home. If you must have a clock in the bedroom, use a small one (generally, the smaller an object, the less energy it has) and keep it away from the bed.

MORE THAN ONE KIND OF NEGATIVITY

Feng shui experts routinely tell clients to keep radios, televisions, and computers out of the bedroom. The primary reason for this is these objects' electromagnetic fields. But these items carry with them another kind of negative chi in the way of information. The bedroom should be a sanctuary of calm, order, and safety, yet television, radio, and Internet news can interrupt this sanctuary with images of violence, misogyny, racism, and other hateful ideologies into the bedroom, which in turn can affect one's mood, poise, and quality of sleep.

KITCHENS

STOVES AND OVENS

In most early cultures the kitchen held a place of special importance: it was used to turn often scarce ingredients into nourishing fuel for a home's occupants. Today, fewer people know how to cook from scratch, and with restaurant and take-out options abounding, kitchens are not used as often as they once were. However, in feng shui theory the kitchen continues to be one of the most important rooms in a home. Symbolically, the kitchen represents a household's health and wealth. For that reason, it is important to create an environment that attracts positive chi. Fortunately, this is easily done: keep the room clean (dishes put away, counters wiped off, floors mopped), quickly repair any appliance that breaks, make sure there is enough light, add a fan if needed to boost circulation, and stick to light colors (white is ideal) to create a feeling of openness.

As a symbol of health and wealth, a kitchens should always be kept clean and properly aerated. A white kitchen, such as this one, is recommended.

It is inauspicious to have a kitchen door (or entryway) facing a bedroom or bathroom door. A kitchen facing a bedroom is considered inauspicious because the cooking smoke can enter the bedroom, disrupting sleep and infusing bed linens with odors. If the kitchen and bedroom doors do face each other, consider constructing a new entrance for one of the rooms. If that is not possible, keep both doors shut at all times when not in use.

A kitchen stove and oven—usually a single combined unit in most homes—represents a very active type of energy. For this reason, it is important to carefully arrange any bedroom sharing a wall with the kitchen. The bed should be placed away from the spot of wall where cooking appliances sit—such close proximity to a stove or oven (even a microwave oven) can affect one's sleep.

KITCHEN SPIRIT

In ancient China, food was often scarce. To ensure abundance, the Chinese prayed to a kitchen god named Zao Wang Ye (king of the stove); his image was placed by the stove in hopes that he would help ward off hunger. Today, Zao Wang Ye remains one of China's favorite mythical deities, and is often honored during the Chinese New Year.

This Qing (or Ching) dynasty (AD 1644–1912) family is setting off firecrackers in honor of the kitchen god. Starting in the Tang dynasty (618–906), the Chinese believed that Zao Wang Ye made annual reports to Heaven on comportment.

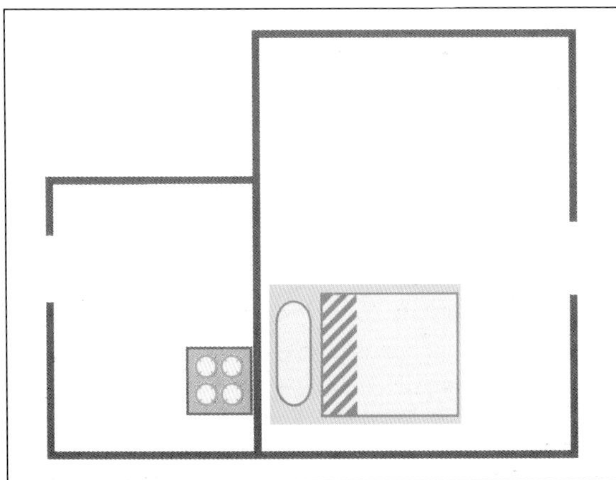

When placed on either side of the same wall, the energy from an oven or stove can impair the sleep of the person in the bed. To fix this situation, move either the bed or the oven/stove. Because many ovens and stoves run on gas which is supplied through fixed gas lines, it may be easier to move the bed.

OVENS AND SINKS

Traditionally, feng shui theory advises against having the sink and stove or oven face each other or be placed next to each other in a kitchen. The sink represents water energy, while the stove represents fire energy, two opposing elements that are said to create disharmony when in close contact. Ideally, the two should be separated by 3 to 6 feet, perhaps with a service area or kitchen island placed between them.

Yet it should be mentioned that the kitchen is the only place where two opposing elements—fire and water—must appear together. The relationship between these two elements demonstrates the Tao of feng shui theory. You may remember reading about the domintation or destructive cycle in chapter 2 (see pages 38–39), in which the element water douses the flames of the element fire. Yet within a well-designed kitchen, a balanced relationship between water and fire helps to create nourishment for a family. This phenomenon reminds people that in feng shui theory, there are no absolutes.

Here, the stove and sink are directly across from each other, separated only by four feet. In feng shui theory, this is considered a moderately confrontational situation.

The ideal solution for the above kitchen would moving the sink area so it is at least 3 feet away from the stove.

REFRIGERATORS

Considering that refrigerators only became widely used in homes in the mid-20th century, they are a rather recent addition to the kitchen. Since they represent cold, they are said to generate yin energy. Like the sink, which also represents yin energy, the refrigerator should not directly face the stove or oven, nor should it be placed near the stove or oven. However, it could be placed near the sink, since the two share the same element—and because this placement makes it easier to wash food after removing it from the refrigerator.

All of this placement advice, however, may mean nothing to the person who has a galley kitchen, one of those tiny spaces found in many city apartments that feature some combination of built-in cupboards, refrigerator, and oven secured against one wall and perhaps the sink, countertop, and more cupboards secured on another. These kitchens—with only an 18-inch walking space between one wall of utilities and the other—typically feature some type of cramped, unpropitious feng shui placement of the oven/stove and the fridge and sink, whether next to each other or facing each other. There will be times when it is impossible to remedy a problem—the best one can do is change what is changeable and keep the room as clean, uncluttered, light, and well-supplied with fresh air as possible.

Another thing to consider when deciding on where to place the refrigerator: in an ideal world, the fridge should not face the door. Feng shui masters believe this can cause conflict between the energy from the entrance door and the energy from the refrigerator, which can lead to disharmony in the family and in financial matters.

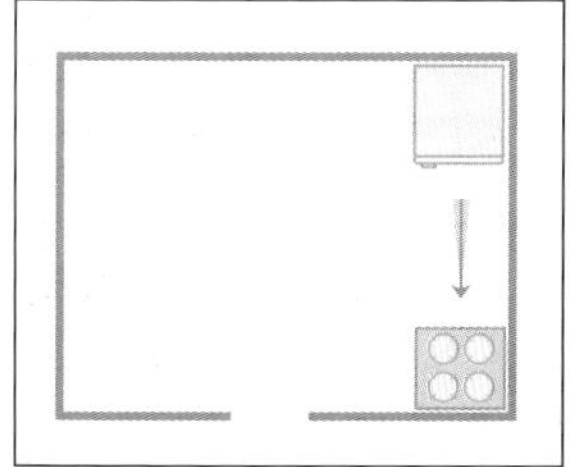

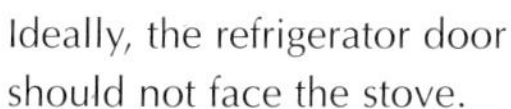

Ideally, the refrigerator door should not face the stove.

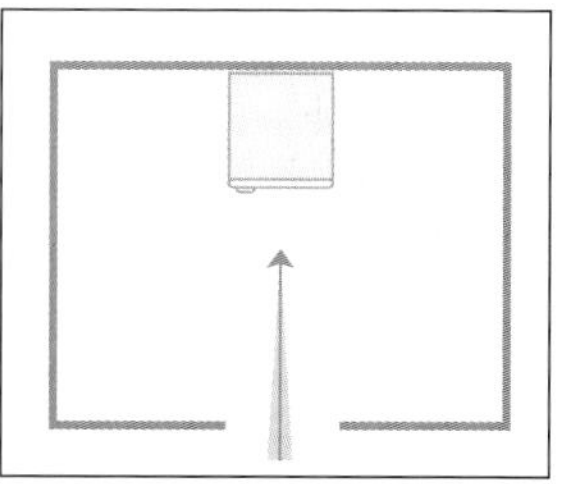

Try not to let the refrigerator door face the kitchen's entrance.

Move the refrigerator, if possible, to another area of the kitchen where it will neither face or sit next to the oven.

DINING AREA

In most modern homes, the dining area is somewhere off the kitchen. As feng shui theorists say, this is a good thing. Such a placement allows food to be served easily and efficiently. In many homes—especially apartments—there is no designated dining area. In such situations, consider choosing an area of the living room nearest the kitchen that is not too close to the front door, which may subliminally encourage diners to rush through meals and leave the home. The space should also be set away from any home office or desk set-up that may share the living room; if that is not possible, a screen or curtain should separate them. The energy from an office is driven and ambitious—not exactly conducive to leisurely meals.

When furnishing a dining room, feng shui practitioners suggest creating a space with a roomy, open feel to foster feelings of abundance. Placing a too-large table, too much furniture, or squeezing the dining area into a small space creates a cramped feeling that discourages positive chi from entering while encouraging negative chi to linger. A cramped space also makes dining less pleasurable than it could be.

Meals would be more enjoyable in this dining area if a screen or curtain was installed to separate it from the office.

TABLE ARRANGEMENT

The dining table seating arrangement is very important for Chinese families, with the elderly given first choice at the table's "best seat"—the chair that is both against a wall and facing the entrance. Many Chinese families arrange their seats according to the occupant's birthdays. To try this, find out your family members' elements (see page 173) and directions (on page 37), then use a compass.

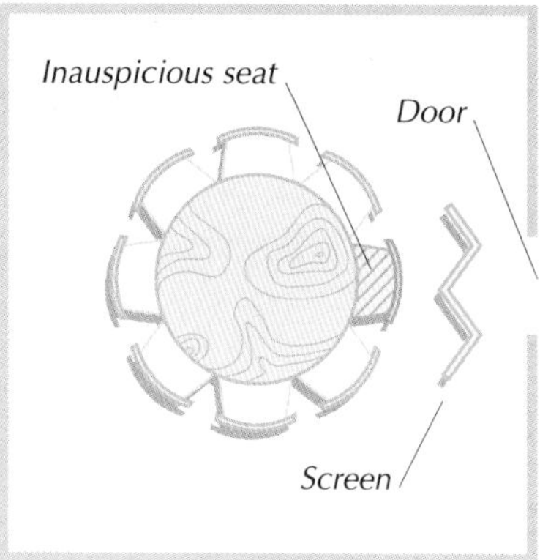

In the above drawing, the most inauspicous seat at the table (striped) has its back to the door. One solution for lessening the seat's negativity is to place a screen between the seat and the door. A mirror hung on the wall opposite the seat allows the chair's occupant to see behind him or her.

The Chinese believe the chair with its back toward the door is the least auspicious seat. The diner can be startled by a person entering the room, or disturbed by drafts.

BATHROOMS

In modern feng shui theory, the bathroom is a home's most yin room. This is due to the room's large amount of exposed water sources: toilet, sink, shower/bathtub. The building materials often used in a bathroom, tile and porcelain, also contribute yin energy. Therefore, yang-enhancing items such as candles, plush towels, and throw rugs are good additions that help balance a bathroom's energy. Interestingly, water symbolizes money in feng shui theory, meaning the condition of this room can affect the wealth of a home's occupants. To encourage auspicious chi to visit the bathroom, the room should be as light, airy and well-ventilated as possible and always kept scrupulously clean.

As in western culture, the toilet has more negative connotations than any fixture in the bathroom; the Chinese believe that the toilet actually produces negative energy, and for this reason. many feng shui practitioners recommend keeping its lid closed at all times when not in use. This is said to prevent negative chi from sucking positive chi out of the home.

Feng shui practitioners have stringent rules regarding where bathrooms should be placed in a house or apartment. Firstly, the bathroom should not be visible from the front door. The positive energy entering the home will be drawn into the sewer lines and dissipated. If the bathroom can be seen from a home's entryway, consider keeping the bathroom door shut at all

Keep your toilet lid closed to prevent posistive chi from being sucked out of your home.

times when not in use, or if possible even moving the bathroom's door to a less visible location.

The bathroom door should also not be facing the bedroom door, or else a bathroom's negative energy can flow unimpeded into the bedroom. In such instances, feng shui masters routinely recommend slightly moving one of the doors. If you are a renter and cannot make changes to the house or apartment you live in, keep both doors closed at all times when not in use.

Another negative bedroom–bathroom situation: a bed's headrest placed against a wall which supports a toilet on the other side. The toilet's negative energy is thought to impair sleep—if nothing else, the noise from any flushing that is done in the middle of the night could disrupt sleep.

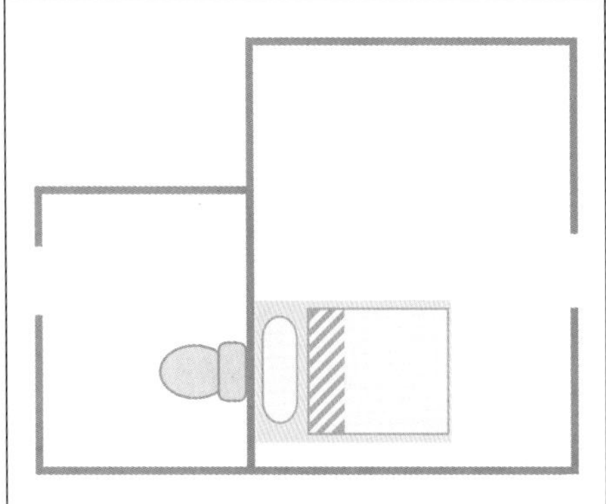

Do not place your bed against the same wall as the toilet.

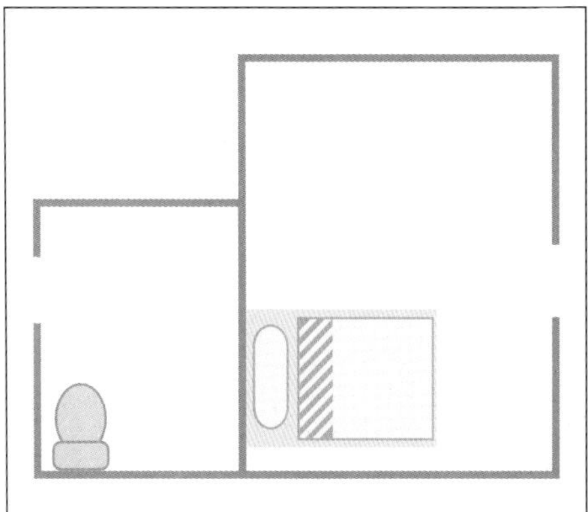

Move the bed or the toilet away from each other. Because it is less complicated to move the bed, consider this option first.

Bathroom and bedroom doors should not face each other. If they do, consider having a new door built for one of the rooms, or keep both doors closed. This bedroom would benefit from having such a door installed.

LIVING AND FAMILY ROOMS

In ancient times there were no living or family rooms. It was not until civilizations moved indoors and began building more elaborate homes that common rooms such as living and family rooms were invented. In feng shui, the two rooms are treated the same, although in America the living room is a more formal room usually reserved for entertaining, while the family room is more of an all-purpose room.

Like other rooms, a living or family room should be relatively uncluttered, light, and airy, with an open feeling. A room that is dark, dank, or crammed with furniture and knickknacks attracts negative chi that stays in the room and stagnates—causing malaise, depression, and money difficulties. Because these rooms are used to entertain both the family and guests, they should be comfortable. Feng shui masters recommend trying furniture, rugs, and art with rounded corners to avoid sharp angles (shars); incidentally, rounded shapes are considered symbolic of money by the Chinese.

Adding light and removing a few pieces of furniture and art would make this room a more relaxing, lucky space.

An airy, spacious, light-filled room such as this is always uplifting and comforting to its occupants.

STUDY, DEN, LIBRARY, OR HOME OFFICE

Not everyone is lucky enough to have a separate room just for work and study purposes. But in homes that do have space for a library or office, it is important that this room be in a secluded, quiet area of the house so that studying and working can go on without interruption. Furniture can be chosen according to tastes—although feng shui masters suggest a mix of squared and rounded shapes to create balanced chi within the room. While some dens suffer from being dark and windowless, with paper-strewn surfaces and stale air, these factors are not conducive to learning or creativity. Clean, free from clutter, plenty of light and fresh air—the Chinese believe these are what is necessary to support the thought process (see pages 146–147 for further details). Chinese homes often feature pictures of mountains, lakes, and rivers on study walls. These images are said to foster creativity and motivation.

This office has an airy, clean feel, an ergonomic desk, and a peaceful view.

DÉCOR AND FURNISHINGS

Feng shui masters believe that each room in a home exerts a different kind of energy. To ensure that this energy is all positive, many suggest furnishing rooms according to each room's use. The furniture occupies the room, serves a home's occupants, and also generates its own energy, making the size, shape, material of individual pieces important.

Depending on the room, furniture should occupy from one-tenth to one-half of a room's floor space. Less than that and a room will look bare and uninviting. More than that and it will look crowded and cluttered. Another thing to consider is proportion—one of the most important concepts in feng shui. A large room should have large-sized furniture; a small room should feature smaller-scale furniture. A piece of furniture that is out of proportion to its environment calls attention to itself, which upsets the harmony of a room and creates negative, unbalanced chi.

Whether a sofa, table, bookcase, or some other piece, furniture comes in many shapes, including square, rectangular, round, and triangular. It should be mentioned that feng shui theory discourages using triangular shapes, which are considered overly aggressive and a source of numerous "poison

In bedrooms, the largest piece of furniture is usually the bed. This bedroom has a good proportion of furniture to floor space; the wood floor and plush blanket make it comfortable.

arrows" (shars). Rather than choose one shape of furniture—say all square or all rounded—it is best to have a balance of shapes, as each shape brings a different kind of energy to the room; too much of one shape can overwhelm a space with one kind of energy.

This glass dining table, metal chairs, and marble floor have a sleek look, but are all "cold" furniture. A table cloth and a rug placed under the table would increase warmth.

Tiles and ceramic are easy to clean but are cold on the feet; here, a rug in the traffic area would help.

FOCUS ON MATERIALS

When furnishing a home, feng shui masters suggest keeping the following in mind:

- Bedrooms. In China, some people rarely wear pajamas, which is why bedrooms are often furnished with an array of soft fabrics and carpets, along with wood furniture (metal is considered too harsh for the bedroom) and wood floors (which are not as cold on bare feet as marble or tile) or carpet.
- Kitchens and bathrooms. These rooms need more cleaning than a home's other rooms, making hard surfaces such as marble, metal, stone, tiles, and so on, ideal. However, these materials can be uncomfortably cold to bare feet, so consider investing in a throw rug for the bathroom or use wood flooring.
- Office/den/library/study. Whatever you call this room, it is preferable to choose a combination of wood furniture and soft fabrics. These create a feeling of comfort and safety which is conducive to creative endeavors.
- Living/family/common room. A multi-purpose room that is used to entertain family and visitors should be kept clean, uncluttered and with a sense of openness. Consider inviting floor treatments such as wood or carpet—tile and marble register as cold and uninviting. Because this room is used by so many people for numerous purposes, it is less effected by chi. This means the owner has more flexibility in decorating it according to his or her taste. Feng shui masters do, however, suggest keeping sharply angled furniture and decorations at a minimum.

COLOR SCHEMES

Traditionally, every culture has assigned meaning to specific colors. Often these meanings are remarkably similar, but more often, a color (such as white) that signals purity in one culture, signals death in another. For that reason, it is important to consider your own reaction to colors when studying the suggestions in this section.

In feng shui, colors are assigned to either yin or yang categories, depending on their yin or yang powers over humans. Primary blue (a yin color) provides a sense of calm , while primary red (a yang color) excites people. Yet add a generous hit of yellow to the blue and you get a yang chartreuse; add a large dose of blue to a red shade and you get a yin violet. Perhaps the easiest way to decipher yin colors from yang colors is this: Within feng shui theory, yin colors are typically cool, yang colors are typically warm.

YIN YANG COLOR CHART

YIN	← NEUTRAL →		YANG
	Green		
Blues Violets Dark Intense Cool	Forest Green Icy Yellow	Chartreuse Hot Yellow	Reds Oranges Light Muted Warm
	Yellow		

Yellow and green can be either yin or yang, depending on whether they are mixed with cool or warm tones.

The warm reds and apricots in this dining room help to increase warmth and appetite.

Adding warm-colored (yang) crockery would balance these blue (yin) accents.

This living room has both yin and yang colors; the fire adds a bit more yang.

COLORS AT HOME

BEDROOM

Not Recommended

Bright, highly saturated colors, especially red or orange. These high-energy colors can cause excitement and make sleeping difficult.

Strongly Recommended

Muted colors such as powder blue, mauve, gray, beige, and neutral colors that have calming, restorative effects and encourage sleep.

LIVING ROOM

Strongly Recommended

Any color an owner finds pleasing. In the living room, groups of people congregate, creating strong positive energy that is not easily effected by outside forces. For this reason, the room needs less protective help from color.

KITCHEN

Not Recommended

Cold colors such as blue or gray are believed to dull the appetite. Hot reds and oranges are fire colors, and thought to create too much heat in the kitchen, leading to burnt food.

Strongly Recommended

White is associated with cleanliness and purity, two factors important to food preparation. White is also a metal color within the five element theory, making it compatible with the kitchen's fire element. Light, warm colors are acceptable.

DEN/OFFICE/LIBRARY

Not Recommended

Bright reds, oranges, and golds are considered distracting to people trying to study, work, or engage in creative pursuits.

Strongly Recommended

Green is considered ideal by the Chinese for soothing the eyes, making it good for the study.

DINING ROOM

Not Recommended

Black is a color that the Chinese consider not conducive to dining.

Strongly Recommended

Colors that are light, bright, and slightly warm, such as salmon pink, peach, apricot, and blush, are thought to stimulate the appetite without overwhelming it.

BATHROOM

Not Recommended

All black or any other dark shade, such as navy blue, burgundy, forest green, or steel gray.

Strongly Recommended

White is an ideal color for the bathroom, signifying cleanliness and purity. Adding yang accents, such as tangerine, chartreuse, or another hot shade, adds a bit of warmth to the bathroom's yin environment.

LIGHTING

Lighting is one of the most practical issues of interior design. If a space is dark, adding a table lamp, ceiling fixture, track light, standing lamp, or some other type of fixture can introduce light. Within feng shui, light is important for attracting beneficial chi to a room. However, there is such thing as too much light—remember, in feng shui, balance is the goal. A room flooded with too much sunlight, for instance, can be hot and uncomfortable. Feng shui practitioners suggest adding a slightly transparent curtain to cut down on a portion of the light that enters the room, or try blinds, which can be adjusted as the sun's position and strength changes.

Work and study areas need sufficient lighting to avoid eyestrain—not overly bright or too dim.

A novel concept to try is using colored light—via a colored light bulb or a tinted lamp shade—to either correct or enhance each room's energy.

LIGHTING AT HOME

BEDROOM

Not Recommended
Direct lighting (bare light bulb)

Strongly Recommended
Indirect lighting (a standing or table lamp, overhead fixture, or light facing the wall—such as a sconce)

LIVING/FAMILY ROOM

Strongly Recommended
Any lighting that pleases the owner.

KITCHEN AND BATHROOM

Not Recommended
Table lamps; cold lighting (lavender, gray, or blue tinted light bulbs or lamp shades)

Strongly Recommended
Warm overhead lighting (red, salmon, or yellow light bulbs or lamp shades)

STUDY/DEN/LIBRARY

Not Recommended
Weak light, low-wattage light bulbs

Strongly Recommended
Bright light, high-wattage light bulbs

DINING ROOM

Not Recommended
Table lamps; weak light, low-wattage light bulbs; overly bright light, bare, high-wattage light bulbs

Strongly Recommended
Moderate spot light over table, chandelier, or candles

MIRRORS

Feng shui practitioners have different opinions about mirrors. Some believe that mirrors can reflect strong energy, while others believe mirrors reflect nothing more than the physical object in front of it. Among those that view mirrors as powerful modern elements within feng shui, it is agreed that they are both helpful and harmful. Mirrors can open up a room by reflecting light and creating a sense of space. While the mirror itself has no power, it can reflect a room's negative or positive chi, making the energy more powerful. For that reason, it is suggested that mirrors be avoided in spots where they can reflect negative energy. Such spaces include facing the front door or facing a bathroom door. Remember that in feng shui, the size of an object typically effects its power. Therefore a small mirror has less ability to reflect energy than a large mirror. Also, the clarity of the glass will affect a mirror's power of reflection: Frosted, patterned or dark glass is less effective at reflecting positive and negative chi than a mirror with clear, unpatterned glass. See page 60 for more information about bedroom mirrors.

This mirror is well-placed in that it does not reflect the bathroom door, and creates the illusion of space.

The smaller the mirror, the less energy it creates, and the less power—whether helpful or harmful—it brings to a room.

FINE ART AND PLANTS

When feng shui masters talk about sculpture, they mean one of two things: "harsh" sculpture comprised of sharply angled pieces of metal, bone, or rock; or "soft" sculpture such as macramé hangings, fabric dolls, and some types of earthenware or rounded wood pieces. Because of their aggressive nature, harsh sculptures should not be placed inside the bedroom, where they can impair sleep. Soft sculptures can generally be placed anywhere, although their potentially yin nature may add too much yin energy to a yin environment like the bathroom.

When selecting paintings or photographs, the Chinese go beyond choosing pieces that match a room's color scheme or décor; they also choose pictures of auspicious subjects. Within feng shui theory, an artwork's subject matter contributes its chi to its surroundings. A Chinese home is likely to display pictures of fish (symbolizing wealth), butterflies (long life), or mountains (ambition and support).

Pictures are effective ways to invite a certain kind of energy into a room. For instance, a dreamlike scene can aid in falling asleep. Of course, such a picture only belongs in the bedroom; hanging it in the study can encourage a person to sleep instead of work.

One more thing to consider, whether siting a sculpture, painting, or photograph: proportion. A large artwork can lend a claustrophobic feeling to a diminutive room, while a single small piece can be distracting—affecting overall chi—when placed alone on or against a large expanse of bare wall.

Artwork and plants can create and stimulate energy in a room, but should be proportionate to the space, as in this studio.

Because plants release oxygen and are living organisms, they are considered carriers of auspicious chi. This makes them an important part of the home. When choosing plants it is important to research species that will work within a given room. Placing a low-light plant on a sunny windowsill may kill it, not an auspicious happening. One must be prepared to look after plants' health; wilted, sick, or dead specimens represent illness and death.

As with artwork, plants should be in proportion to the room they are used in. For instance, a small pot of African violets is out of proportion to a cavernous living room, while a potted bamboo will overwhelm a small bathroom. Shape, too, is an important consideration. A plant with a squat, rounded shape might be perfect for balancing chi in a room with many pieces of tall, angular furniture, while a spindly, vertical plant is ideal for introducing the element of height to a room with low, rounded furniture.

A terrace garden brings auspicious chi to this kitchen without crowding it, while the tall plant adds balance with its height.

RELIGIOUS ITEMS

From Catholic crucifixes or Buddhist figures to Jewish mezuzahs, in cultures the world-over it is common to find home decorations that reflect a homeowner's religion. These items can bring comfort or spiritual energy to the home. They can also lend a protective element, helping to deflect negative energy when placed in the entry facing the front door or on the doorpost.

However, these items attract strong energy that can impair sleep and should not be placed in the bedroom—over the bed is an especially bad place for them. Nor do religious objects belong in the bathroom, where they may be overwhelmed by negative energy. The kitchen's fiery energy can fight with an icon's spiritual energy, making the kitchen another inauspicious location for such art unless it depicts a Chinese kitchen god (see page 63).

Jewish mezuzah

Confucian ancestor scroll

Christian cross

Islamic prayer beads

Buddha

Shiva statue

Shinto God figurine Daikoku

CHAPTER FOUR

FENG SHUI FOR THE HOUSE

SITING, LANDSCAPING, AND EXTERIOR AND INTERIOR DESIGN CHOICES ALL RELATE TO THE FLOW OF CHI.

BUILDING LOCATIONS

Consider the time, money, and effort most people go into finding, purchasing, and maintaining their houses. Looked at that way, it makes sense to do everything possible to create a healthy, happy home with the resources available. In Chapter 3 you read about general guidelines that can be applied to any living situation. Here, we offer specific information to individuals or families living in houses.

INAUSPICIOUS LOCATIONS

WHERE NATURAL DISASTERS OCCUR

An area pummeled by rock slides, hurricanes, or tornadoes; somewhere prone to floods; a site near

This home could easily be damaged by flood or hurricane.

Canyons often have stagnant air and harsh topography.

Rolling valleys have good air circulation and gentle terrain.

a faultline—these are all potentially dangerous areas to live. Feng shui is concerned with safety, making these locations extremely unlucky. If you live in such an area, there is nothing you can do to change the region itself. Therefore, you must pay special attention to what you can control, such as your house's siting, structure, and landscaping.

AT THE BOTTOM OF A CANYON

A house built at the bottom of a canyon is subject to falling rocks, floods, and stagnant air. Feng shui masters also point out that beneficial chi may not reach a home situated on a canyon floor. A more propitious housing site would be a valley, among small hills.

DIRECTLY ON TOP OF A MOUNTAIN

Mountaintops are windy places that are continually assaulted by moderate and strong gusts. In this environment precious soil is blown away, plants have trouble growing, and favorable chi is pushed past a house without giving occupants a chance to benefit. A better site is the base of a mountain or among small hills.

Mountaintop homes have amazing views, but are exposed to strong wind and cold.

INAUSPICIOUS LOCATIONS (CONTINUED)

WITH A HOME'S ENTRANCE FACING A MOUNTAIN OR HILL

In feng shui, towards the base of mountains and hills are considered lucky places to build homes. However, these sites become unlucky when the house is built with the entrance facing a nearby mountain or hill. These natural landforms possess strong chi that can press down on an entrance and overwhelm a home. If you live in such a home, move the entrance to the side of the home that faces away from the mountain.

A home's entrance should not face a nearby mountain.

FACING A PRISON, MENTAL HOSPITAL, OR OTHER CORRECTIONAL FACILITY

Homes should not be located near correctional facilities.

Much of feng shui is concerned with avoiding natural hazards. The Chinese view any type of correctional facility as both sources of extremely negative energy and human hazards. It is difficult to fully secure a correctional institution, leaving a small but always-present chance that a violent or unstable person could escape and harm individuals living nearby.

FACING A MILITARY BASE OR POLICE STATION

Police stations are buzzing with sirens and constant motion.

Though military bases and police stations are concerned with maintaining peace, the process is chaotic and noisy—disturbing calm and impairing the smooth flow of beneficial chi.

AN ENTRANCE TO A CITY

Tunnels, bridges, and freeway offramps—wherever cars, buses, and trucks rush into a city, so does noise, crowding, and pollution. The energy created from this influx is considered mixed and unpredictable—not the kind of energy good for creating a pleasant, healthy home environment. If you live near a city entrance, consider installing double windows, keeping windows that overlook the scene curtained, and moving your front door so it does not face the traffic.

FACING A CHURCH, SYNAGOGUE, OR OTHER RELIGIOUS BUILDING

A religious edifice has strong chi.

Religious buildings exude a strong spiritual chi. While this is not a bad thing, it is not necessarily something you want to live near. Powerful spiritual energy can overwhelm the energy in your home that enhances health, wealth, family, and luck energy. If you are in a home facing a religious building and do not wish to move, consider moving the front door to the side of the house and keeping sheer curtains on those windows overlooking the religious building.

Busy bridge traffic and its associated energy could create too much yang energy for a home.

ORIENTATION

When feng shui practitioners talk about orientation they are referring to what direction a home or other building faces. Houses should generally avoid facing the direction where the winter wind is generated—though this direction differs depending where in the world you live. For example, a home in Ohio is buffeted by winter wind from the northwest. Winter wind is cold and can lend a chilly, sluggish energy to a house. If you are in the market for a new house, orientation is something to think about; however, there are remedies for poor orientation in your existing home. What feng shui masters mean when they say a home faces a certain way is that its front door is facing a given direction. This is why one of the easiest remedies for poor orientation is to move the entrance door out of the path of the winter wind. If this is impossible, consider planting some type of windbreak with dense bushes or trees, or construct a fence to weaken the wind's power. Or, install a vestibule with a outer door and inner door at the entrance.

Because it offers the most solar energy, southern exposure is considered ideal in most moderate climates.

AUSPICIOUS SITUATIONS

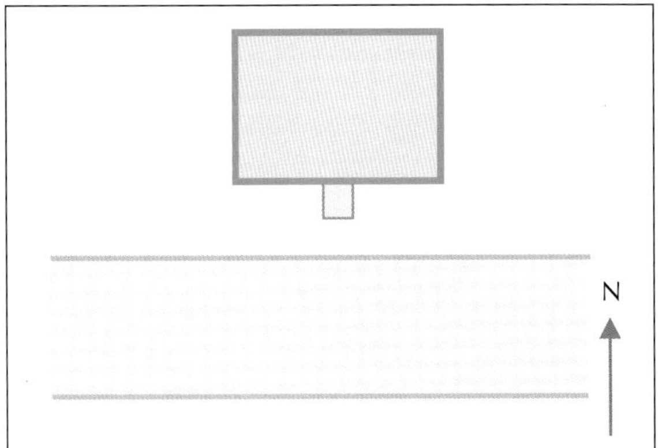

A house with southern exposure is able to avail the life source of the sun.

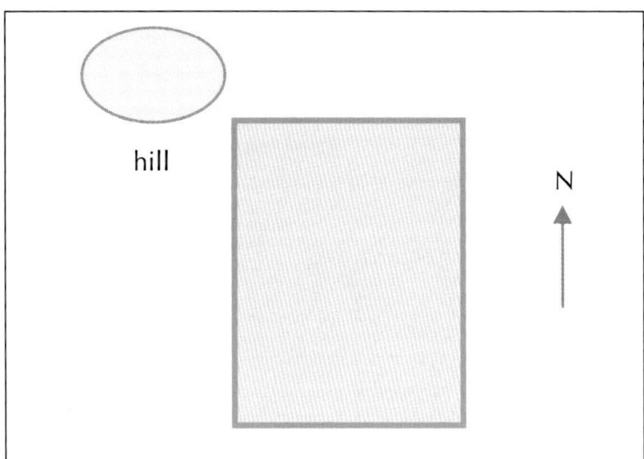

This house is protected from the winter wind by a hill on its northwest side.

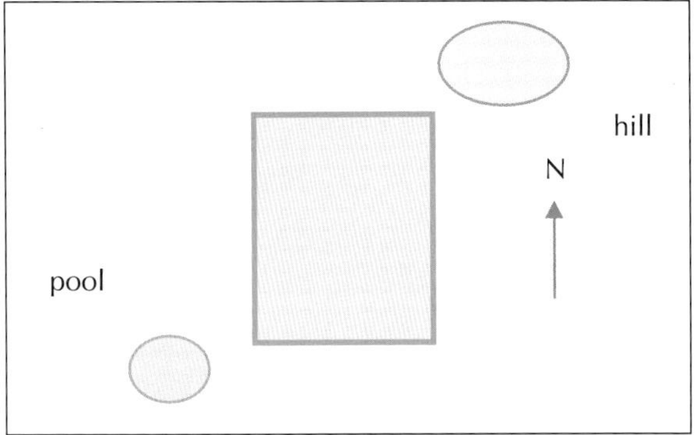

A house located in America's southwest or midwest is cooled by a pool or pond placed in the path of the southwestern summer wind. The hill on the northeast corner helps retain auspicious chi for the house.

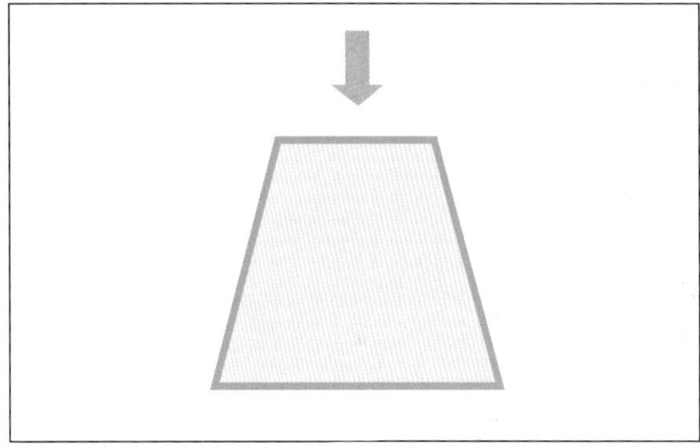

In feng shui, if one portion of the house is narrower than another, place the door at the narrow end. This helps to keep auspicious chi from leaking out of the house.

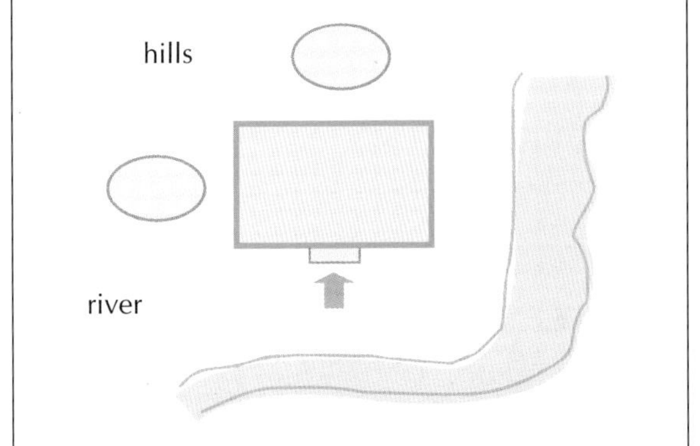

This house is cradled by a river and hills on two sides. The river brings a continual supply of fresh chi while the hills help hold the auspicious energy in and around the house.

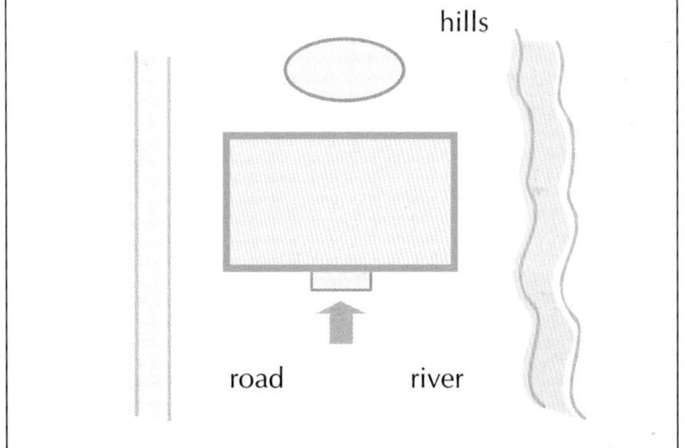

This house was built on a site with a road on one side, a river on another side and high hills at its back. This is a classic example of good feng shui.

ORIENTATION (CONTINUED)

In China, it is considered inauspicious to live surrounded by graves. In addition, the Chinese would never place a home between a body of water and a graveyard. To do so, creates an inauspicious mix of chi from the water and chi from the deceased. (Interestingly, a few feng shui experts contend that it can be beneficial for commercial buildings to face a graveyard.)

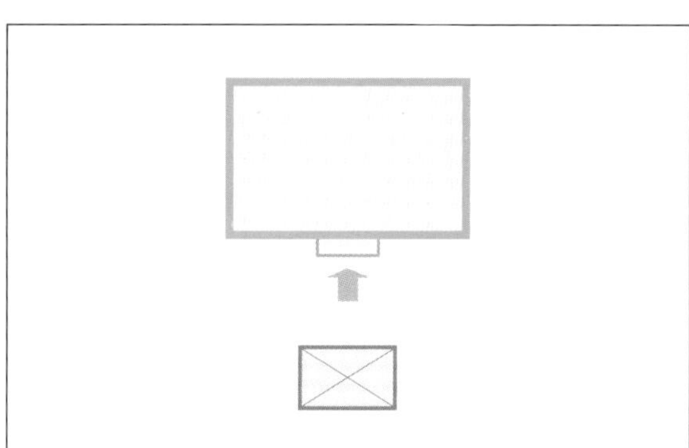

Do not place a garage, shed, or other outbuilding directly in front of the house; it might block incoming auspicious chi.

One of feng shui's concerns is the safety of a home's occupants. A home with stones, clutter, or other hazards in front of the house is said to be visited by negative chi.

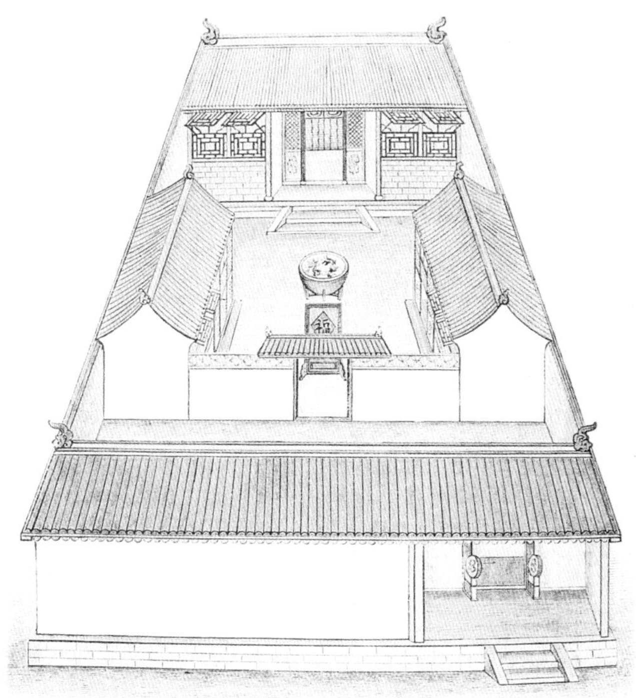

This illustration depicts the layout of a typical Chinese home designed according to the tenets of the Form School. Homes such as these have been built in China for the last 1,000 years, and many still exist today. The house is layed out so that the flow of chi is optimized: the door is in one corner (typicallt to the southeast), the toilet area is enclosed and on the far right of the entrance. A second entryway leads to a courtyard flanked by two buildings; perhaps containing rooms for two daughters. The back of the building houses the main living area and the master bedroom, in the most protected location at the rear. A feng shui master might use the Compass School theory to determine the best location for the front entrance according to the birthdate of the owner.

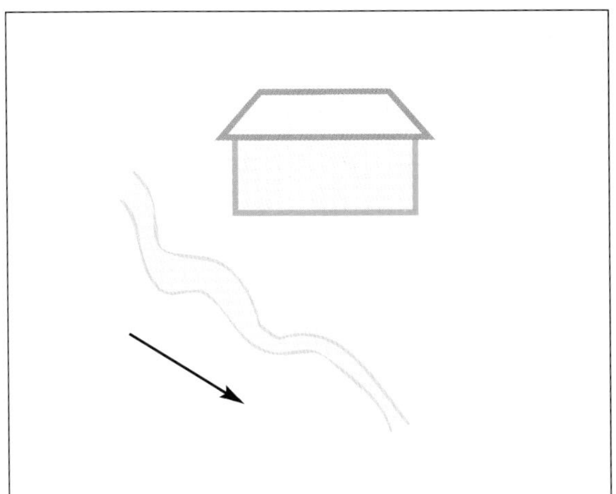

In China, the preferred route of water and traffic is moving towards the house rather than flowing away from it. It is believed that the latter option—as in the inauspicious example above—leaches energy from the house, thus affecting the wealth of the household.

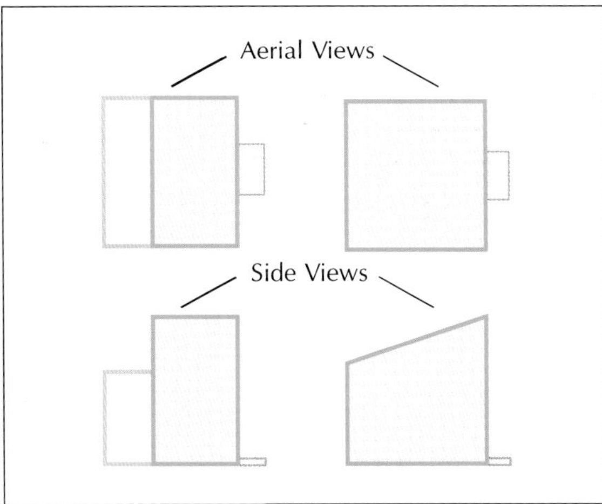

Both homes above feature the bulk of their height on their entrance sides. According to feng shui, the entrance should never be located in a tall portion of a house because this forces the chi to travel downward to the rest of the house instead of exanding into the entire building. If a house features multiple heights, it is better for the chi to start low and move higher.

WIND AND WATER

Feng shui means literally "wind water," hinting at the early Chinese's reverence toward these important elements. With that in mind, it is not surprising that the best feng shui location to build a home is near mountains (which the Chinese view as the ultimate wind block) and some body of water.

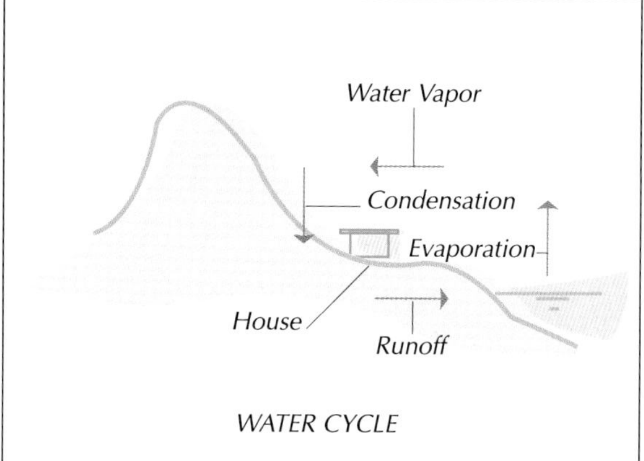

The base of a gently-sloped mountain is considered an especially lucky place to build a home—even more lucky when a body of water is near to help cool and refresh the air.

WATER SOURCE

Back in the early days of feng shui, one of the guiding principles of the practice was building near a suitable water source—usually a gently moving river. Today, few homeowners know exactly where their municipal water comes from. Yet, this is important to know. Modern feng shui practitioners suggest studying local cancer rates, having water tested for chemical and microbe levels, and studying a house's water pipes before purchasing a home. If you did none of this before buying your home, consider at least installing filters for the water you drink and bathe with.

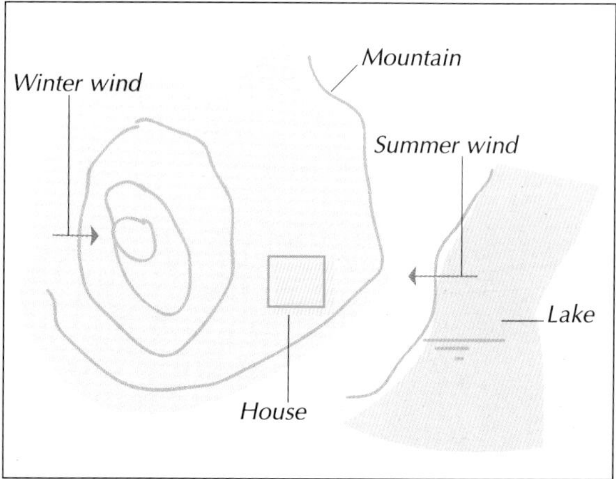

Here, a mountain blocks the winter wind, while the summer wind is made more a few degrees cooler and more refreshing after crossing a lake.

Determining a good feng shui location is often a matter of common sense. The homes above are embraced by a cool, clear body of water and protective mountains—as well as the natural beauty of the environement—a very auspicious situation.

ROADS

Few people are lucky enough to own homes that sit beside a meandering stream or river. What most homeowners have is a house that sits alongside a road, which in modern feng shui theory is the same thing as a river. And, just like a river, the best kind of road to live near is a gently curved street with moderate traffic. Such a road is said to carry auspicious chi at a pace that is easily absorbed by the houses along its path. An avenue with fast-moving traffic carries chi too quickly by a house, while a street that is choked with slow-moving traffic will deliver stagnant chi.

Negative chi can also be delivered by shars (see page 50), which carry bad luck and are said to produce maladies ranging from irritability to marriage problems to financial ruin. A shar can be caused by anything that points at or travels toward you or the space you occupy, although the most common shar associated with a house is a straight road pointing towards a home's location. This usually occurs when a house is built at a T-bar junction or at the end of a cul-de-sac. A row of trees or bushes or a fence placed directly in front of the house can help deflect a shar's "sting."

Auspicious Situations

In ancient China, waterways were both a source of water and a means of travel. Today, with municipal water systems, it is no longer necessary to live near water, and roads and cars have to a large extent replaced rivers and boats. This is why in modern feng shui roads are symbolic of waterways—and both are treated in the same manner.

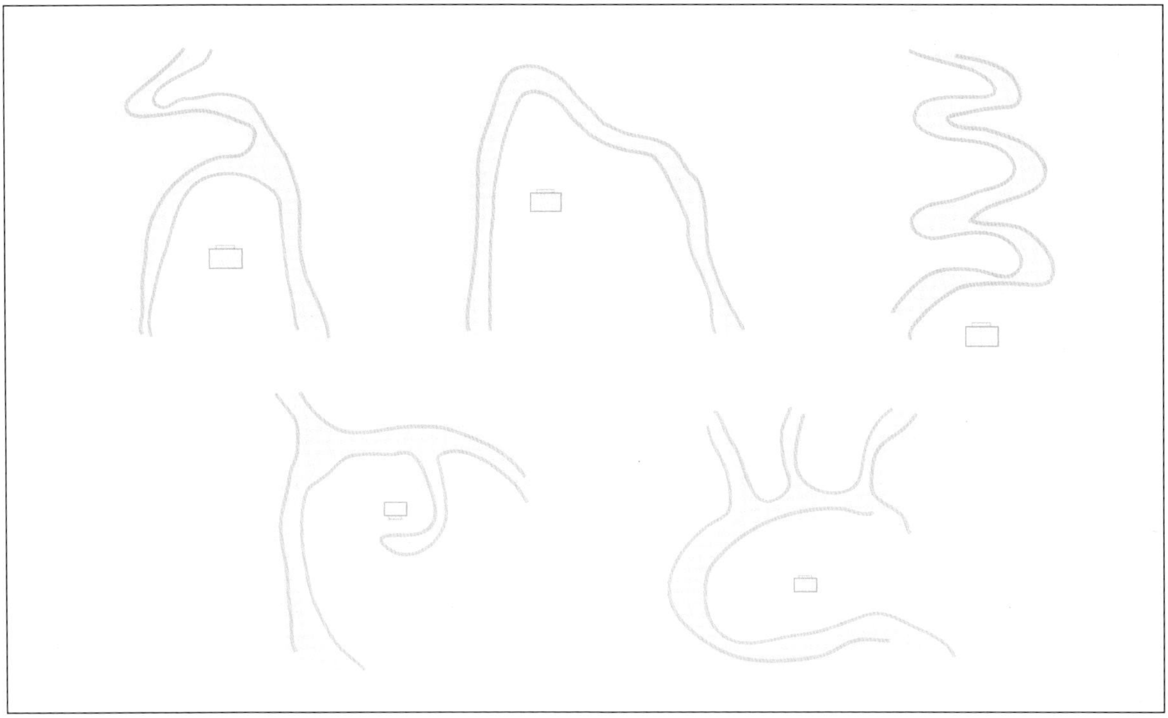

The five homes above are hugged on three sides by roadway—they are almost surrounded by beneficial chi.

Similarly placed home hugges on three sides by rivers would be beneficially affected.

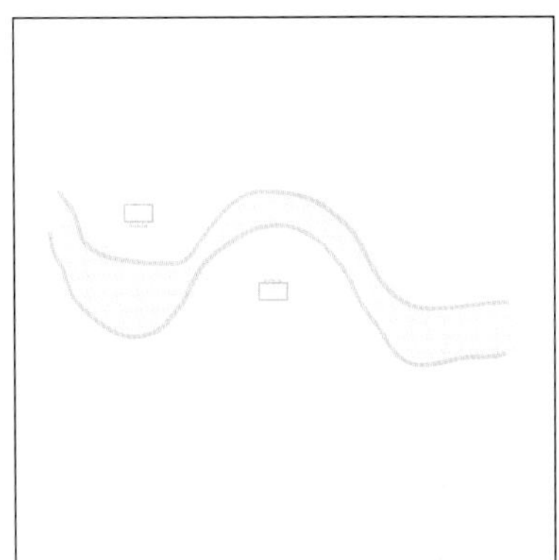

These homes, cradled by the roadway above, are thought to be built in especially auspicious locations since they are embraced by the road's beneficial chi.

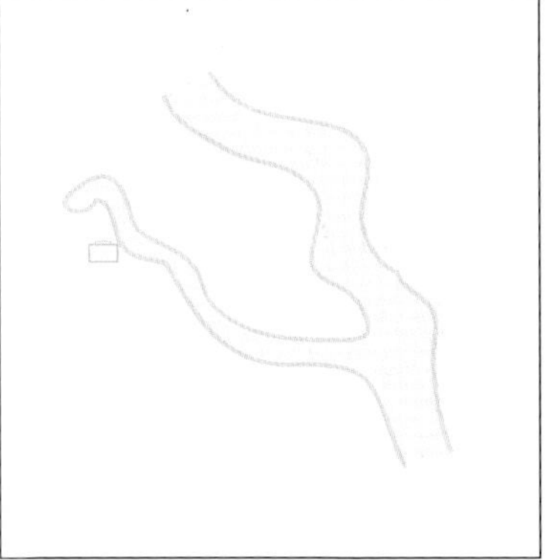

A waterway or roadway should not point directly at a home, which the Chinese consider to be a shar. The above home is in a safe location, away from the tip of the offensive shar

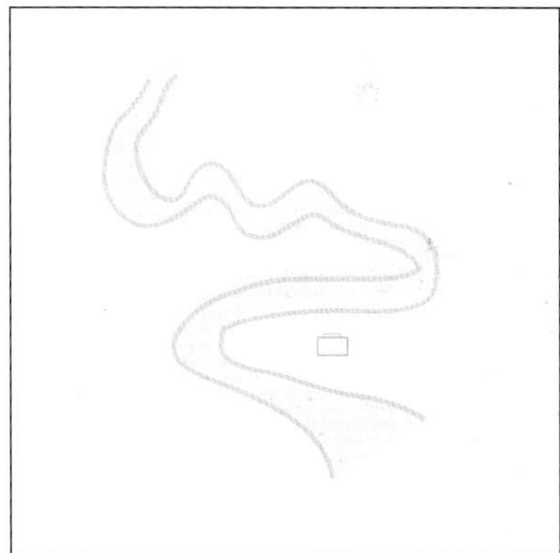

In ancient China, homes were built inside a river's or stream's bow. Placing a house on the outer part of a bow was considered dangerous— if a river overran its banks the house would become flooded. Today, it is also considered dangerous to build on the outer curve of a road—a fast-moving car may not be able to maneuver the turn and instead may crash into the home.

ROADS (CONTINUED)

INAUSPICIOUS SITUATIONS

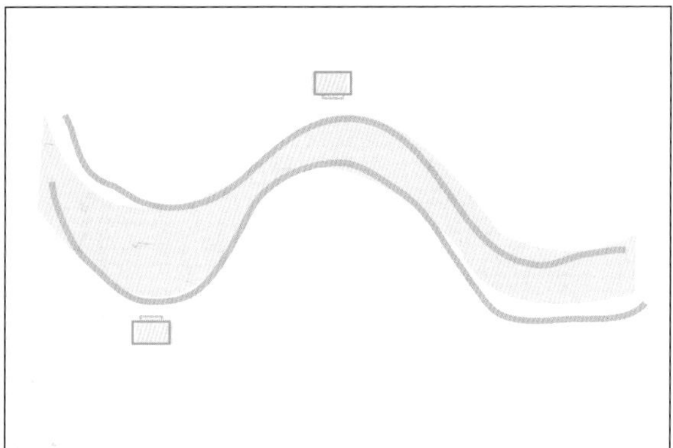

A home located on the outer curve of a road is vulnerable to hits from out-of-control drivers. A better location would be inside a road's curve. Fast-flowing chi on the outer curves also damages these locations.

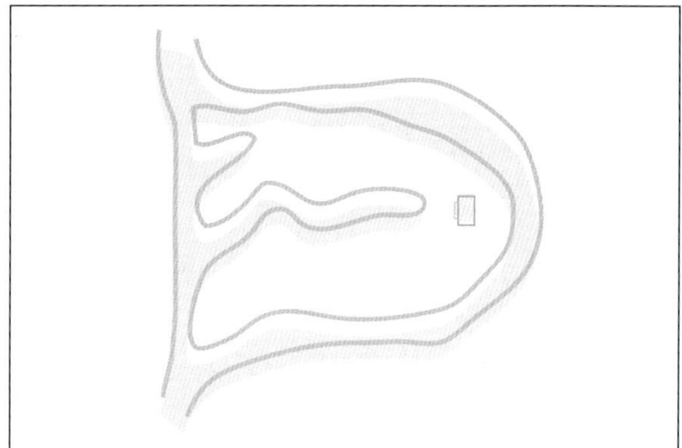

Too much of a good thing: To be surrounded on all sides by either rivers or roads is considered inauspicious in feng shui because lucky chi does not have a way to emter. In the example above, there is also a road or waterway pointing directly at the home, creating a poison arrow.

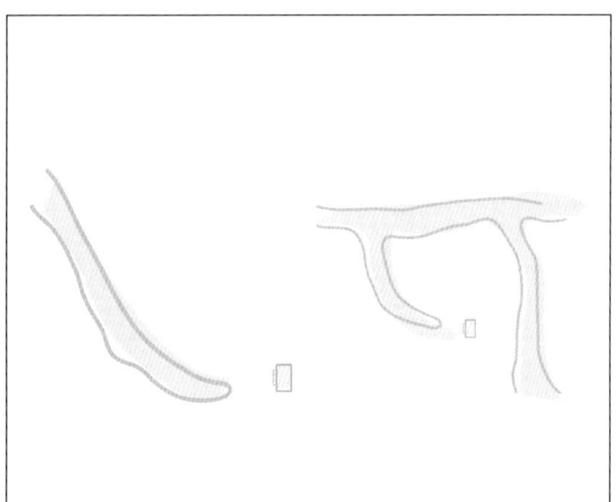

A road aiming directly at a house (at the end of a cul-de-sac, for example) is considered extremely unlucky. This situation is known as a poison arrow or shar, and it delivers a large dose of aggressive negative energy directly to the home. A better location would be alongside the road.

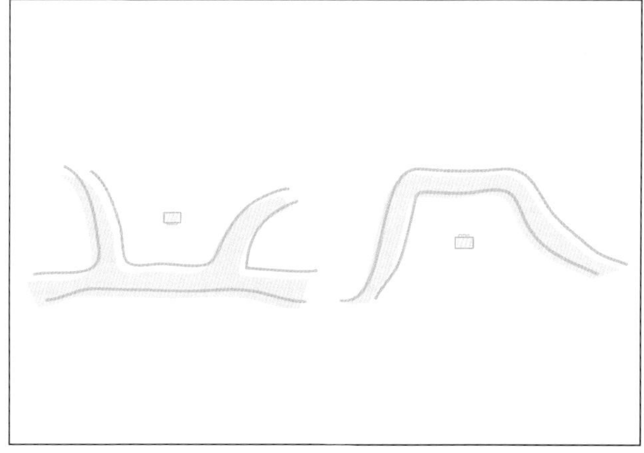

In the two examples above, homes are built near busy freeways and highways. While it is considered beneficial to live near a moderately used road, it is unlucky to live near busy, noisy, highly trafficked roads. Highways and freeways are said to bring chaotic, aggressive chi upon a home.

LOT SHAPE

A lot's shape can affect the home that sits on it. The most favorable plots are those regular in shape: square, rectangular, or oval. These shapes attract a good balance of chi. Avoid lots or fences that are triangular, trapezoidal, or other shapes with narrow portions. If the narrow portion of the lot is at the front, chi will be choked on its way in and out of the lot. If the wide portion of the plot is at the front, chi will escape too readily. If you currently live on such a lot, try correcting its shape by installing a fence, hedges, or trees to create a square or rectangular lot. If you feel it is wasteful to have unused land, plant flowers on the portion of the lot that falls outside the fence or hedge.

A square, rectangular, or oval fence can help an irregularly shaped lot maintain more even chi flow. Trees or hedges can also be used.

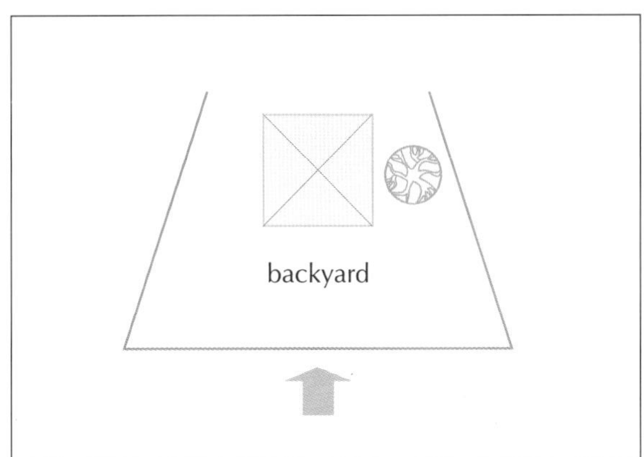

This triangular lot's narrow neck chokes chi, making it difficult for energy to flow.

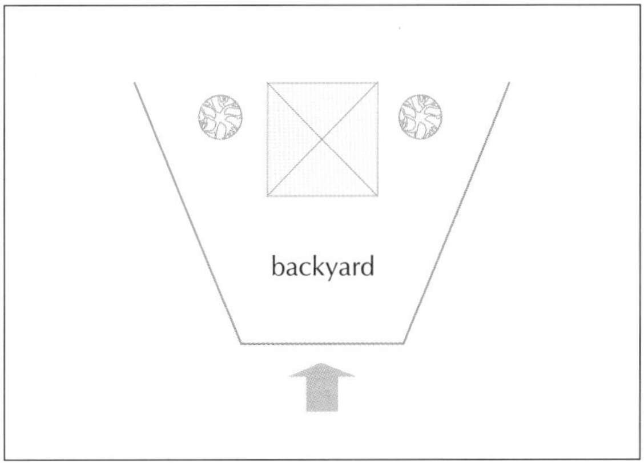

The wide entrance to this lot causes chi to escape the property without benefiting the home and its occupants.

GARAGES AND SHEDS

Most modern suburban homes are built with garages attached to one side of the house, with an interior door connecting the garage and the kitchen, dining room, laundry room, family room, or hallway. Rural homes may have a garage a few yards away from the home or behind the house. Some people use their garages for the family car, others for storage, and still others convert them into workshops. Regardless of where a garage is located and what it is used for, general feng shui principles apply. To keep a garage from pulling chi away from a house, it should be in proportion to the house. A large three-story home needs something bigger than a narrow structure that barely houses one car, while a two-bedroom home should not have an elaborate two- or three-car garage.

The garage door should be wide enough to allow a car to easily pass through. A narrow garage door makes it difficult for both the family car and helpful chi to enter, while an overly wide door allows beneficial chi to escape.

Not all homes have sheds, the diminutive cabin-like outbuildings used to store gardening tools, lawnmowers, and other landscaping equipment. In terms of size, feng shui treats sheds like garages—they should be proportional to the house.

Admittedly, garages and sheds are not often associated with neatness—yet a clean, uncluttered space is vital for creating good chi. In feng shui it is believed an oil-puddled space cluttered with tools, boxes, and other items creates negative chi that can affect a homeowner's health. From a practical standpoint, a garage's or shed's disarray can be a health and fire hazard. To remedy the feng shui of a disordered garage or shed, one must keep the floor free from grease and oil, remove all unneeded items, and install shelving and cabinets to hold tools, and other stored items.

To prevent chi from being pulled away from the main house, a shed must be smaller than the garage and located unobtrusively to the side of the garden or against the house.

DRIVEWAYS AND FRONT WALKWAYS

If there is one rule to follow when positioning a home's driveway and front walkway it is this: Avoid poison arrows! A poison arrow occurs when the driveway or walkway is laid down in a straight line pointing directly at the door. These poison arrows deliver a strong dose of aggressive negative energy straight through a home's entrance. If you have either a walk or a drive that is a poison arrow, the best remedy is to tear it up and create a gently curved path that is not aimed directly at the front entrance.

The straight pathway pointed at this house delivers negative energy right to the front door. A smaller or unpaved path would have less impact, but a curved path would be best .

A slightly curved front walkway creates an auspicious entrance to this home.

ENERGY FACTORS

In feng shui there are two sets of rules often used to judge a house's feng shui. Called the strong five and the weak five, these were developed by the ancient Chinese as a way—in addition to geographic location, structural shape and building material—to determine the energy of a home. More specifically, these guidelines help a feng shui master ascertain a living space's positive strong (shi) and its negative weak (hsu), which in turn helps a practitioner knows where to focus his or her efforts.

THE WEAK FIVE

The five weak are five areas feng shui experts look at when deciding on a home's overall feng shui. If any of these are present, a feng shui expert makes special efforts to eliminate them, remedy them, or strengthen the overall chi of a home in other ways.

1. A large house with few occupants. Westerners like the space and privacy a big home can bring, but from a feng shui standpoint, a small family, couple, or single person in a large house is not good: The small amount of energy generated by a few people is not enough to fill a large house, and negative chi will rush in to fill the empty space. If more people cannot be invited to live in the house, feng shui practitioners might suggest adopting pets, or applying classically yang elements to the house, such as brighter light, warm-colored interiors, carpet, and plush-covered furniture.
2. Small house with a big door. A large door placed on a small residential building lets wealth-enhancing chi leak from the house into the surrounding environment, where it benefits no one. If your front door is too large, or if your entrance consists of a double set of regular-sized doors, it's important to install a smaller door to keep chi from escaping.
3. Neglected exterior. Tall weeds, a messy lawn, a car on blocks in the driveway, chipping house paint—an unkept exterior creates a look of poverty, which the Chinese believe can actually affect your finances. If the exterior of your home is rundown, there is only one way to remedy the situation: Fix it up!
4. Improperly designed or dilapidated kitchen. In ancient China, the kitchen was a home's most essential room. Without a well-designed kitchen, raw ingredients could not be transformed into nourishing meals. Moreover, ingredients were expensive in China, so it was vital that a kitchen be designed well so food would not be burned or otherwise ruined. Also, because fire, sharp knives, and slippery surfaces were—and still are—unavoidable in kitchens, the room represented something of a danger. An orderly, well-lit, and efficient kitchen helps ensure a cook's safety.
5. Small house with a big yard. A small house that sits on a large lot or has an expansive garden, big swimming pool, or elaborate garage is a house that is losing its chi. If a home's external factors are larger or showier than the home itself, chi will be drawn out of the home and to the showy thing outside. The Chinese believe a home which cannot keep its chi will deliver misfortune to its owners.

THE STRONG FIVE

The strong five are powerful magnets for beneficial energy. If these factors are present, a home is believed to have good, positive chi—despite any feng shui flaws in a home's location, layout or design:

1. A small to medium house with many occupants. In many Western cultures, a palatial home is a common homeowner's goal—even if a home has just two or three people to fill it. Feng shui, however, suggests the opposite. In China, it is common for a couple and their child to share a two to four-bedroom home with grandparents, an unmarried uncle, a widowed great aunt, young newlyweds and others. People—as long as they are good, positive people who get along with each other—create good, positive chi. This beneficial energy fills every corner of a smaller home, helping all who live there. In ancient China it was believed that the more positive people energy a home had, the less room there was in a house for evil spirits to enter. Note that cleanliness and orderliness are important within feng shui. To best benefit from positive people chi, it is essential to keep a home uncluttered and relatively dirt-free.
2. A house with a small door. While feng shui stresses the importance of proportion, a door that is slightly on the small side is widely favored because it is believed to keep wealth-enhancing chi from leaking from the home. A commonly-used analogy is that a smaller door is like a closed wallet—wealth cannot escape it. On the other hand, a standard three-foot wide door on a three-story house is too small, and creates a tight, miserly, stagnant environment within a home.
3. Well-kept exterior. If you could remember only two rules of feng shui, perhaps they should be these: Positive chi hates a mess and neatness always attracts auspicious energy. An unkept, overgrown front yard, a poorly painted house, a grease-soiled driveway, a dirty front door—all of these things create the appearance that a home's owner has lost control of his or her finances, which in turn can cause an owner to lose control of his or her finances. From a practical standpoint, an unmaintained exterior can present safety hazards for a home's family and its visitors.
4. A home with pets. In feng shui theory, pets are like people: they generate positive chi. Several animals in a small home—say two animals in a two-bedroom home—create enough positive energy to crowd out any negative energy waiting to enter. Pets represent an especially important way to generate positive chi among single people and small families, or larger families who live in big homes. Be aware, however, that animals must be treated kindly and kept healthy to generate this auspicious chi. Mistreating an animal creates very negative chi in a home and can bring bad luck to the pet's tormentor. Also, because cleanliness is important, pet owners should make special efforts to keep a home neat.
5. Water running towards the southeast. In ancient China people had no plumbing and instead used rivers and streams to carry waste away from their homes. Because the southeastern portion of China is closer to sea level than the central and northern areas, water running toward the southeast carried waste safely away without contaminating a home's personal water storage. Today, with modern sewage and municipal water supplies, this rule is not applicable the way it once was. But for tradition's sake, many feng shui practitioners still honor it.

FORM OF THE HOUSE

When feng shui masters talk about the form of a house, they are referring to its shape: Is it round, square, rectangular, or a more irregular shape? Positive chi likes square, rectangle and round houses best, because these shapes make it easy for auspicious energy to enter and circulate unhindered. Homes with more irregular shapes—think L, H, and T shapes—make it difficult for chi to move around freely. Furthermore, irregularly shaped homes have "missing corners," or "missing directions" according to the pa kua (see page 33). A house that is missing a corner will lack the type of luck symbolized by that corner.

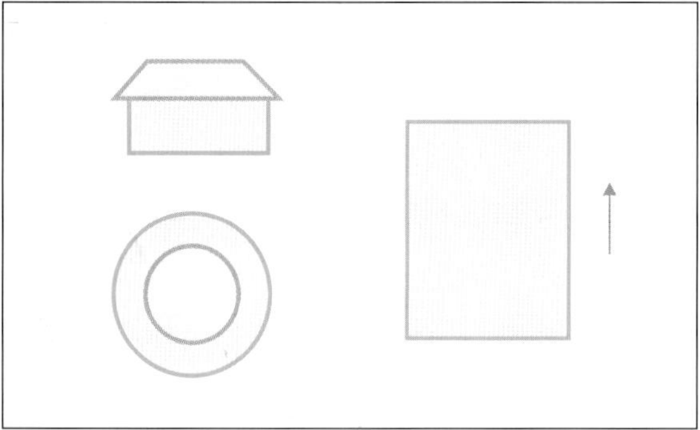

Above, a traditionally shaped square house, a round home, and a rectangular shape. These are auspicious forms because they encourage chi to circulate in all corners of a home.

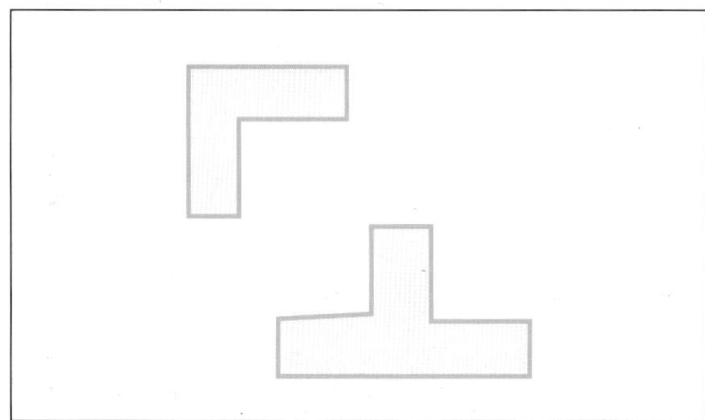

Irregularly shaped homes—like the examples above—have "missing corners," which can lead to short-term or long-term misfortune for the owner.

While it's best to avoid irregularly shaped homes, there are things you can do "build in" the missing corners. A row of hedges can be planted around the home to create a square, rectangle, or circle. A fence, garden sculpture, or trees can also be employed for this purpose.

Facades and the Five Elements

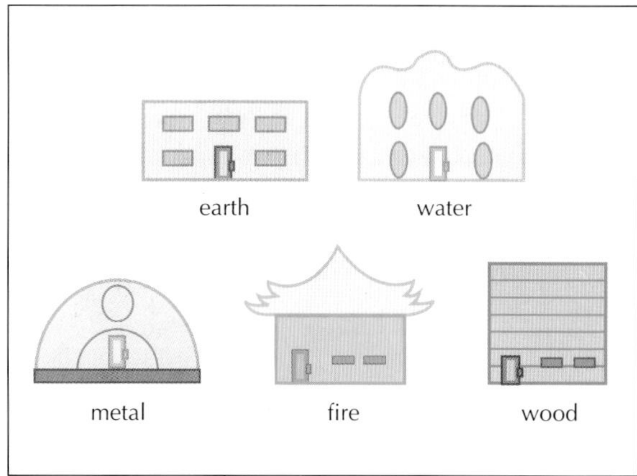

The five element theory (see pages 172–173 to determine your element) can also be applied to the shapes and building materials used for house façades, as shown above.

BUILDING WITH YIN AND YANG

When feng shui masters judge a home's balance of yin and yang elements, they look first at the façade. In China, this important design element is compared to a human's face: it is what an onlooker sees first. A home's façade can be curved (yin) or muscular (yang); it can be subtle (yin) or bold (yang).

Building materials can be also categorized as yin and yang. Yang materials such as wood, adobe, and brick conduct less heat than yin materials like metal, glass, stone, or cement. In a house built of yang materials, people are less affected by outside temperature changes, while those in a house built of yin materials suffer more from extreme hot or cold. Central air-conditioning and heating can help regulate temperature but involve added electricity and cost to your home. On the other hand, increasing the wall thickness and building with layers of material (blanketing a layer of air) will add insulation to a yin-material house.

Yin Materials

metal and glass

brownstone

stone

cement

Glass, stone, metal, and cement are all "cool" yin materials.

Yang Materials

wood

brick

adobe

Wood, brick, and adobe are "warm" yang materials.

WHERE IT GOES

A place for everything and everything in its place. No, the old adage is not an official feng shui rule, but it could be. When it comes to room placement, feng shui has definite ideas about the best locations for bedrooms, living rooms, bathrooms, and kitchens.

It is important to note that there are two schools of thought with regard to the Southern Hemisphere. One maintains that as the seasons are reversed, so should the directions. The more traditional view is that the compass does not change direction as you cross the equator, and so (despite climate) feng shui rules for direction and location should not change either.

KITCHEN

In the northern hemisphere, a northern location is ideal for the kitchen. The north part of the house does not get the heat of more southern spots, and heat from the kitchen helps warm cooler parts of the house in the winter without overheating the house in the summer.

A kitchen located in the northern part of a house can help balance the energy of a home.

A bathroom should not be placed in the center of a home, but in a hallway preferably in the northern portion of a house.

A living room should receive enough sunlight and warmth to harmonize the energy between people and objects.

BATHROOM

For privacy, the bathroom should never be placed in or near the middle of a house. A better site is off a side hallway, preferably with a northern orientation (southern areas should be reserved for living room or bedrooms).

LIVING ROOM

In most places within the northern hemisphere, the south gets the morning and early afternoon sun, making southern rooms a few degrees warmer than northern rooms. Therefore, a living room or family room will feel most comfortable when oriented toward the south. Of course, people living in hot desert areas such as the southwestern United States may want their living rooms cooler than other rooms. For this reason, they may wish to place common areas in the northern portion of the house.

WHERE IT GOES (CONTINUED)

MASTER BEDROOM

According to the pa kua (see page 33), the center position is associated with prestige. For this reason, the Chinese like to place the master bedroom in the center of a house, far away from the front door and the living room, where it is sequestered from family member's comings-and-goings and outside elements. Many westerners, however, may feel that a master bedroom in a home's center is a too exposed place. If this is the case, a secluded southern portion of the house is considered by the Chinese as the next best option.

BEDROOMS

Children's and guest bedrooms do best where there is some sunlight, making the south, southeast and east good locations.

WINDOWS

In China, southern windows are considered very important from an energy standpoint. Allowing morning sun to come in through southern windows warms a home in winter, saving energy and making for a smaller electric bill.

A master bedroom requires privacy and should never be placed near a home's entrance, where people are constantly coming and going.

Children's bedrooms should be placed near the master bedroom for close supervision, while bedrooms for teens or grown children should be situated farther away to afford both parents and older children a bit of privacy.

Windows facing south or southeast should be larger, while ones facing north should be smaller. As a practical consequence, this will help to reduce heating costs.

TREES

Trees are highly prized in feng shui theory for their ability to block negative chi, attract good luck, and to indicate fertile soil. From an environmental perspective, trees are welcome for the fresh oxygen they manufacture, which in turn makes air easier and more pleasant to breathe.

As a general rule, smaller trees can be grown anywhere on a property; larger trees should be kept away from the front door where they can block the entrance of beneficial chi. Also, do not build over the tree roots, which may eventually damage the home's foundation. Within the northern hemisphere, the ideal location for larger trees is typically the northern part of a lot, where they can block the cold winter wind that comes from the north. Individuals living in hot desert areas may wish to grow big trees on the southern part of their property, where the trees can filter out a portion of the region's harsh sun.

When planting trees or building a home on a tree-studded lot, be aware that a tree becomes inauspicious when one or more of its main branches points directly at a door or window. This is called a poison arrow or shar, and it

When using trees against the front of the house, opt for specimens that are shorter than the house and be sure to leave plenty of room on each side of the front door so beneficial chi can enter. Also, the front door should not open directly towards a large tree trunk.

Trees planted in front of the house should not crowd the entrance. This creates a claustrophobic feeling and makes it difficult for beneficial chi to reach the front door.

delivers a strong jolt of negative energy directly into a home. Fortunately, tree shars are easily corrected by pruning the offending branch or, if the tree is young, training its branches to grow in a different direction. A tree's branches should not rest upon a home's roof. Not only is this dangerous during windy or icy weather, it creates a sense of pressure among residents.

Branches of a big tree like this should be kept away from the house.

DESIGN ELEMENTS TO CONSIDER

According to feng shui practitioners, these common design elements can attract inauspicious chi if treated incorrectly:

SPIRAL STAIRWAYS

For good feng shui, it's best to avoid spiral staircases, which in China represent a downward spiral toward death. If you must use such a staircase, situate it in a corner next to a wall. A spiral staircase is considered especially unlucky when in the middle of the room because it is said to create a vortex which pulls a room's energy down into the death direction.

FIREPLACES

While they bring yang energy into a home, fireplaces also produce smoke, which in feng shui is akin to negative chi. If a home is well-ventilated and a fireplace's chimney, flue and hearth are kept clean, a fireplace can be very helpful—especially if placed in the portion of a home hit by frigid winter winds. Although many modern homes and cabins have fireplaces situated in the middle of the living or family room, feng shui masters prefer that a fireplace be placed against a wall where its strong energy does not create an imbalance of chi within a home.

A spiral staircase is considered especially inauspicious when placed in the center of a room, where it can drain away positive chi. (If you must have a spiral staircase, minimize its inauspiciousness by placing it in a corner against a wall.)

Because they generate strong yang energy, fireplaces should not be placed in the center of a room, where they can disrupt a space's balance of chi.

COLUMNS

In feng shui columns are treated much the same as beams: As things that block positive chi. Columns, like beams, are believed to create an oppressive, hostile environment that can lead to dishonesty, bickering, and headaches among a home's residents. Fortunately, there are ways to remedy a column, including "hiding' it by wrapping it in cloth, placing plants or a bookcases or a mirror in front of it or on it, or putting a screen around it.

Hanging a soft sculpture from a column or placing a plant in front of a it are two ways to minimize a its negative power.

SKYLIGHTS

Anything that lets in light and air is considered good within feng shui. But, because of their ceiling position, skylights are not recommended above a bed, where they can make a sleeper feel conspicuous, on view, and insecure. To create a feeling of security wherever a skylight it used, it helps to use tempered, shatterproof glass and install a skylight curtain that can be drawn at those times you want privacy. Because proportion matters in feng shui, a skylight should not be too large, otherwise too much of a room's energy will be exposed to outside forces.

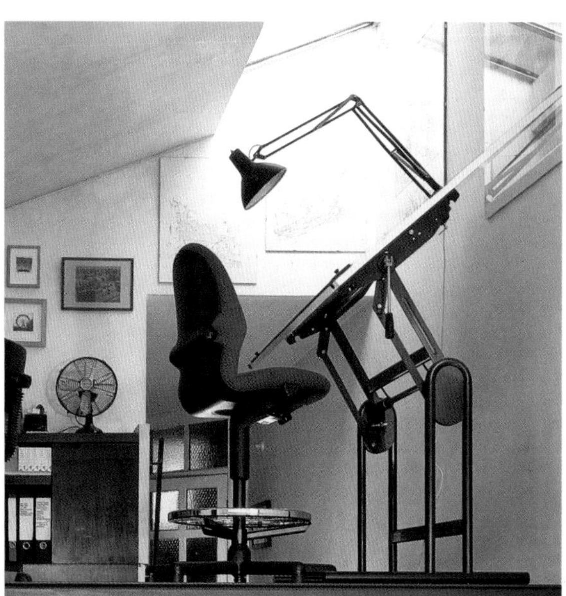

A skylight can be a nice addition to a living room, family room, or study; however, they are best kept out of the bedroom.

CASE STUDY
HOME ENTRANCE

The new owners of this home wanted both the exterior and interior of the house redesigned. They were also interested in applying feng shui principles to the house and surrounding landscape, which include a swimming pool, guest cottages, a pond, and tennis courts. This is a lot of property and energy to manage, but the feng solution was simple: focus on the house's entrance.

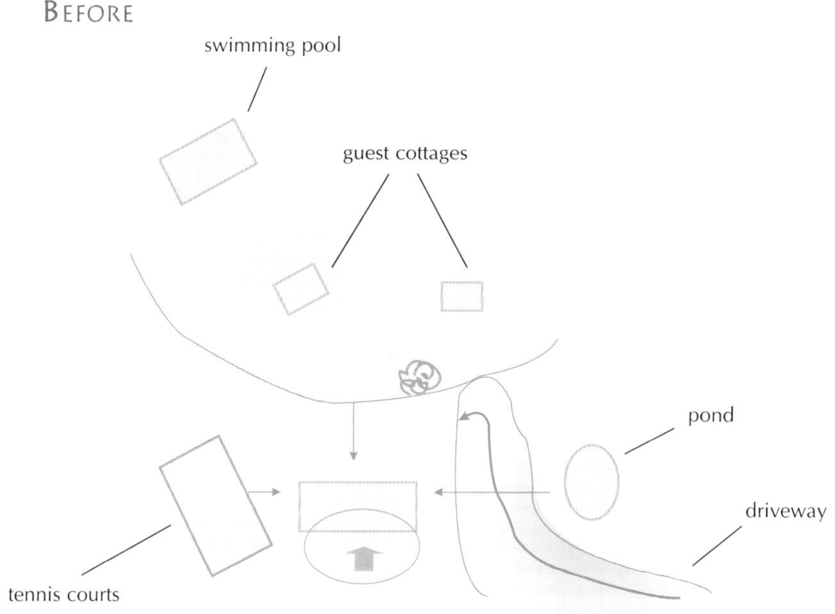

The primary problem with this home is the flow of chi. Because the driveway leads to the home's back door, chi enters through the home's back door, meaning the back of the home gets a large dose of chi. The sides of the home also receive chi from the cottages, swimming pool, and pond located on the sides of the house. Because the home's circulation is not good, the incoming chi never makes it to the front of the house. To make matters worse, the front of the house, including the front yard, are not well-kept, giving chi even less of an incentive to visit. The result is an imbalance of chi which can lead to financial loss, impaired health, and misfortune.

After

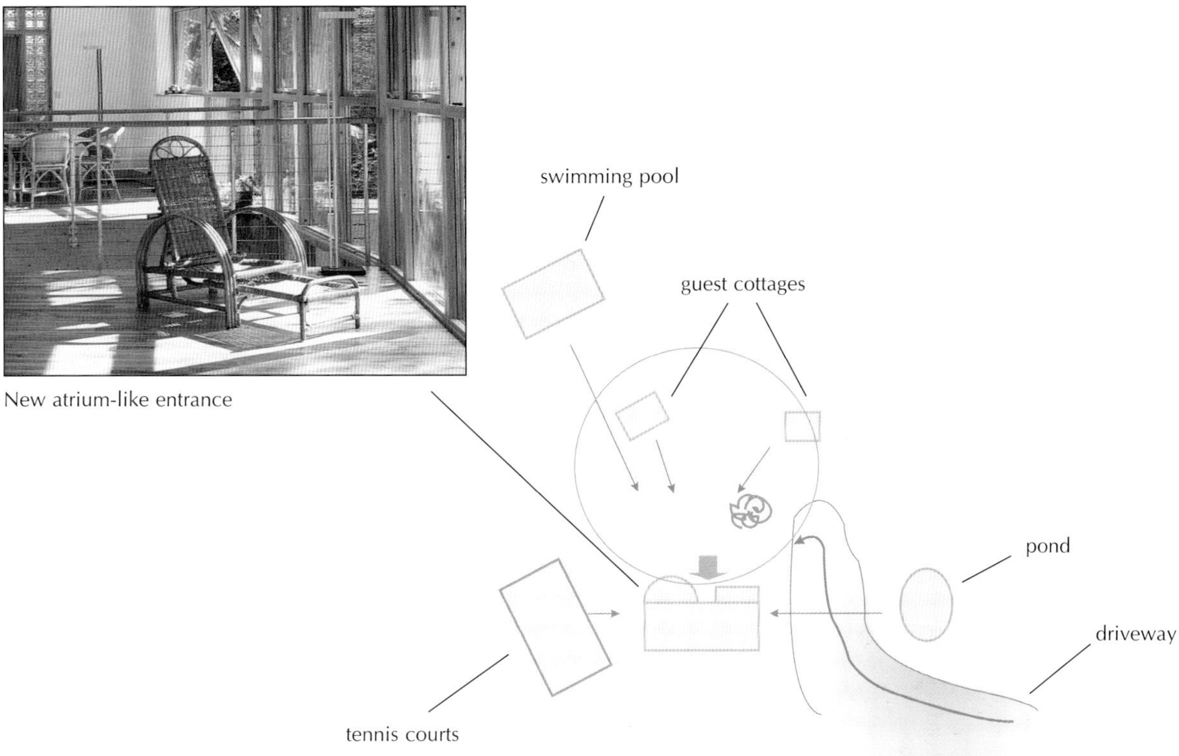

New atrium-like entrance

To remedy the flow of chi, the back door—indeed, the entire back of the house—was re-designed as the front of the house, while the house's original front yard was re-landscaped as a back yard. To encourage chi to linger in the new backyard, attention was given to plants and flowers, and a new meandering pathway was laid between the backdoor and pond. Note that this is only a start; there is still room for further improvement in the backyard. The land between the pond and the house can be further developed with plants, lights, or a bridge, and something (such as a sculpture or bench) should be placed between the back door and the tree (closer to the tree) to block the tree's potential shar.

CHAPTER FIVE

FENG SHUI FOR THE APARTMENT

FENG SHUI'S BASIC PRINCIPLES ARE AS EASILY APPLIED TO URBAN LANDSCAPES AS THEY ARE TO RURAL SETTINGS.

CITY LIVING

Feng shui's roots are decidedly rural: The people of ancient China did not have the resources or technology to erect large, elaborate structures to fend off the sun, wind, inclement weather, drought, and other natural elements. Instead, they looked to naturally occurring forms—such as mountains, hills, and rivers—to keep them protected and comfortable. Considering its beginnings, feng shui theory may seem out of place in modern cities. Not so.

In modern cities, the mountains that ancient Chinese once named "dragon mountains" are represented by skyscrapers that are called "main mountains." The chi-boosting rivers and streams that were so auspicious in early times are still auspicious in today's cities, yet they are as likely

In cities, bridges over water are considered "heaven dragons," while tunnels are characterized as "earth dragons."

The term "main mountain" signifies the tallest mountain in a region area, or in the case of a city, the tallest building.

FENG SHUI AROUND THE WORLD

BEIJING: The city of Beijing was built in strict accordance with feng shui theory. Not only is the city surrounded by mountains, a canal was built to protect the town's borders. A second, smaller canal also runs through the Forbidden City, applying its positive water element to Beijing's interior.

LONDON: With numerous water elements and many bridges (heaven dragons) and tunnels (earth dragons), London benefits from an all encompassing smooth energy flow.

PARIS: With its array of concentric arrondissements, Paris' energy is concentrated and held tightly within its center0most districts.

SYDNEY: With its chi-welcoming harbor, Sydney attracts a smooth flow of energy. The Sydney Opera House acts like a main mountain, guarding and protecting the city's chi.

to be actual waterways as they are roads and avenues—both act as symbolic rivers in modern feng shui.

In Manhattan, the Empire State Building and the Twin Towers are considered "Main Mountains." Flanked by rivers to the east, north, and west (and the ocean to the south), Manhattan has plenty of its own chi-enhancing waterways, yet the city also boasts many streets and avenues. Furthermore, New York City's many bridges are called "heaven dragons" by modern feng shui practitioners, while the city's many commuter and subway tunnels are considered "earth dragons." Dragons symbolize extreme luck within feng shui; with so many heaven and earth dragons—as well as strong main mountains and plenty of riverways— Manhattan benefits from being one of the best feng shui cities in the world.

URBAN DWELLING

THE APARTMENT BUILDING

In chapter 4 we discussed feng shui for houses. While houses are common in suburban and rural areas, they are rare in true cities. Whether the city is Paris, Hong Kong, Moscow, or another urban center, chances are its residents live in apartments. Generally speaking, the apartment building can be considered on a par with a house, governed by the same principles. From a feng shui standpoint, a building with good chi is one that gets plenty of sunlight, is not flanked by taller buildings, and is on a block that is protected from strong wind.

NEARBY ROADS

In feng shui theory, curved, meandering rivers are considered ideal because they carry chi at a pace that benefits the structures on its banks. A curved street with moderately gentle traffic is the urban equivalent to the meandering river. An apartment building situated on such a street will be touched by its smooth-flowing chi, creating a good living site. Yet many cities are designed in grids with straight roads, and instead of gentle traffic, feature a mad rush of commuter cars, taxis, delivery trucks and buses. If you live in such a city and have your choice of apartments, find a building located on a quiet street— according to feng shui principles, a relatively calm environment outside the apartment will help create a sense of calm inside.

When looking for an apartment, try to find a building on a street with slow-moving traffic to reduce exposure to noise.

In today's tight real estate market, however, few people have the luxury of finding a suitable apartment located on a peaceful street; if you are one of the many city dwellers who live on a busy street, it is even more important to create tranquility within the apartment. To cut traffic noise, consider installing double-glass windows, using a white noise machine to muffle street noise, and keeping windows closed during times of heavy traffic and relying on a fan to circulate air.

Another street-related concern is the possibility of a poison arrow, or shar (see page 50). This occurs when an apartment building sits directly across from an on-coming street. If such a building is the only space you can afford or find to live in, avoid apartments in the front of the building that face the poison arrow; living units at one of the building's sides or back are less affected by a shar's negative chi. If you must live in one of the units facing the shar, feng shui remedies include asking your landlord to install a fence (to help block the negative energy), or plant a row of bushes in front of the building (the shar's negative energy will be greatly absorbed by the plants). Another option: installing window boxes with moderately tall (one-foot or taller) plants in each of your apartment's windows to help absorb the shar's inauspicious chi.

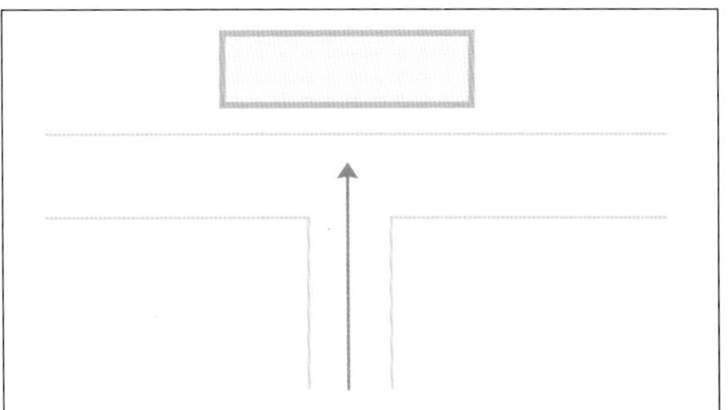

The oncoming road, above, is called a poison arrow because it shoots negative chi directly at the structure in its path. Those apartment units facing the shar will be most affected by its inauspicious energy.

SOLUTION:

One feng shui remedy for deflecting a poison arrow is planting trees or bushes in front of the building to absorb the shar's bad chi. In addition, the vegetation will also serve as an air filter for pollution.

BUILDINGS NEAR A SUBWAY ENTRANCE

Living near a subway entrance exposes you to an "earth dragon's" lucky chi.

Most of the world's great cities feature some kind of underground train system. Known as subways, metros, or undergrounds in various cities, these trains are called "earth dragons" in modern feng shui and are believed to deliver extremely auspicious "dragon chi" throughout a city. Individual street entrances to underground trains are known as "dragon mouths." Living near a dragon mouth is considered extremely auspicious because it is where an earth dragon exhales its lucky chi into the surrounding environment, thus saturating local parks, businesses, and apartment buildings with favorable chi.

Living across from a dragon mouth or on the same block as a dragon mouth is lucky, however, living in a building that is located directly over a dragon mouth is not lucky. Why? Feng shui masters explain that living directly above an earth dragon means putting up with train vibrations and noise. The train's shaking and clamor causes disharmony, negating any benefits one gets living near an earth dragon. What if the only building you can afford to live in, or the only building you like, is located directly above a subway? Choose an apartment unit as high in the building as possible—the further away from a train's rumbling and shaking you are, the less affected you will be.

BUILDINGS NEAR PARKS

In many cities, apartments located next to or near a park cost considerably more than a comparable apartments that are surrounded only by blocks and blocks of other buildings. Humans instinctively feel more comfortable near nature, and knowing this, building owners price their apartments accordingly.

If you consider the feng shui benefits of an apartment near a park, its higher price might just be worth it. As you have already read, feng shui's reverence of nature was born of necessity: early humans relied directly on nature to create shelter, provide food, and lend a feeling of calm to their living spaces. Though modern humans have air conditioners to regulate a room's temperature, ceiling fans to circulate air, and furniture and floor coverings to create a comfortable environment, feng shui continues to imbue nature with restorative powers; thus living near a park will always be considered "good feng shui." Scientifically speaking, a park's large concentration of plants and trees creates a continual supply of fresh, clean oxygen, making air in parkside apartments less stale than their city-bound counterparts. A park's greenery also creates a feeling of calm, which benefits those living nearby.

Individuals fortunate enough to choose what side of a park they live on, would do well to consider their city's climate. According to feng shui theory, if the cold winter wind travels down from the northwest, a building located on the northwest part of the park is a less desirable spot than the southeast area of the park. Each building has a different feng shui reading depending on which side of the park it is located on.

Living near a park is very beneficial; for as long as cities have had parks, parkside real estate has been coveted.

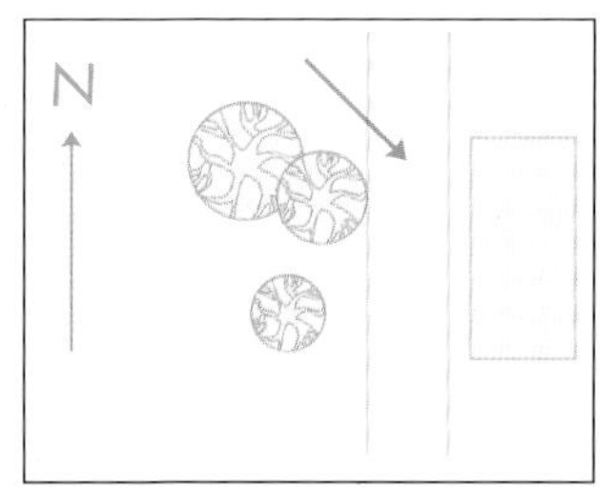

Because this apartment building sits in the winter wind's path, its location is slightly less favorable from a feng shui standpoint than a building located out of the cold wind's way.

A cool southwest wind keeps an apartment building pleasant in the summer, making this location highly favorable.

BUILDINGS NEAR RIVERS

A city that boasts a moderately slow-moving river is blessed from a feng shui point of view. Whether the river flanks the city or travels through it does not matter: the waterway works to distribute auspicious chi to all structures near it. This is why it is especially fortunate to live in an apartment building located near such a river. If you happen to be lucky enough to choose what side of a river to live on, take a moment to find out where your area's harsh winter wind and the cooling summer wind come from. Note that these directions vary depending on where you live; a city in southeastern America will get its winter wind from a different direction than an urban center in the northwest, for example. An ideal location is one that is not directly hit by cold winter wind, but is in the path of the cooling summer wind.

If you live near water, there is one thing to be aware of: According to Chinese medical beliefs, morning dew can cause arthritis. The Chinese believe that if a nearby body of water creates a heavy morning dew, the house's or apartment's bedroom should face away from the water. If that is impossible, the bedroom window should remain closed during the night.

Bodies of water are extremely auspicious in feng shui, even more so than parks; Hong Kong reaps great benefits from ocean breezes.

MAIN ENTRANCE AND LOBBY

An apartment building's main entrance opens directly to the outdoors, just as a house's entrance does. Like a house's entrance, an apartment's entrance should be in proportion to the building's size: A large entrance on a small building will allow beneficial chi to escape while letting unlucky chi slip in; a small entrance on a large building will constrict the entrance of beneficial chi while simultaneously trapping inauspicious chi within the house.

The strong façade design around this small entrance make it seem larger, helping to attract positive energy to the building.

Many apartment building entrances are equipped with two sets of doors separated by a small vestibule. From a chi standpoint, this is ideal. The vestibule restrains good interior chi, slowing it down so it cannot quickly escape the building. From a practical position, double doors help insulate a building's ground floor against bitter weather.

An apartment building's lobby serves the same purpose as a house's entry or foyer: It slows the escape of propitious chi while making it harder for inauspicious chi to enter. Visually, the lobby serves as a cushion between the very private realm of the apartment and the very public city street just outside the door. Feng shui masters suggest paying close attention to a building's lobby when searching for apartments. Is the lobby's size in proportion to the building's size? Is it inviting? Is there good circulation of air? Is the temperature controlled? Is the space kept clean and uncluttered? Is it in good repair? Are the lobby's colors neutral and comforting? For individuals trying to remedy the feng shui in their existing lobby, feng shui masters suggest studying the above criteria, then discussing appropriate changes with your building's manager or co-op board.

Front courtyards (such as this one) and vestibules slow down the good chi entering the building, encouraging it to linger.

WINDOWS AND TRAFFIC

In an urban setting, traffic—from cars, trucks, buses, and motorcycles—generates an enormous amount of noise. So much noise, in fact, that people living on busy corners and avenues often report feeling irritable, frustrated, and aggressive; in feng shui theory, all of these conditions can be attributed to high noise levels. Ideally, a city dweller will avoid apartment buildings located in traffic-congested areas. In the real world, however, urban residents may not have the luxury of choosing an apartment according to the neighborhood's traffic levels. If you are among those individuals who live on or near a busy street, it is imperative from a feng shui standpoint to reduce the noise coming into your apartment. Excess noise is considered extremely serious because it severely disturbs an apartment's chi, and in addition to the conditions listed above can cause headaches, depression, anxiousness, and insomnia.

Ways to soften noise levels include installing double windows to insulate the apartment against noise, using a white noise machine to muffle street noise below, getting a desktop water fountain to add a soothing-sounding water element to the environment, playing tapes or CDs of ocean sounds for more soothing water sounds, and blocking sound by wearing ear plugs.

Double-glass windows and heavy curtains work together to insulate an apartment from harsh traffic noise below.

ROOM WITH A VIEW

Anyone who has ever stood at an apartment window looking at the city below or the sky above knows the value of a view. Feng shui masters believe an expansive view gives the apartment "space to breath." Furthermore, a good view can create a sense of well-being and calmness among apartment dwellers, as well as generate auspicious chi within the apartment itself. Because a poor view inhibits positive chi (as well as sunlight), a bad view is attributed with anxiousness and depression. What makes a view bad? Feng shui masters categorize bad views as follows:

An expansive view can drain chi from your apartment. Try to affix a mirror to the inside of the window or hang curtains.

TOO MUCH VIEW

Yes, there really is such thing as too much of a good view—it is when a window is too large and the view stretches without interruption to the horizon. This situation is akin to an overly large front door: it leaks an apartment's beneficial chi into the environment. To partially remedy the solution, a small inward-facing mirror can be attached to the inside of the window to reflect beneficial chi back into the apartment.

A RELIGIOUS BUILDING IN VIEW

In many western cultures it is considered good luck to look out onto churches, temples, synagogues, or other religious buildings. Not so in China, where a religious building is said to saturate a house or apartment with its spiritual chi, which in turn chokes off other types of beneficial chi needed for health, wealth, romance, children, and luck. If one of your windows overlooks a religious building, consider instailing sheer curtains that will block the view and still allow sunlight into the room.

ACROSS FROM AN ACTIVE INDUSTRIAL CHIMNEY

Chimneys regularly spout soot, dust, and chemicals into the air, making them bad from a health standpoint. Within feng shui, these pollutive elements also represent negative energy, making

Views from apartments located in crowded cities—or in cities with narrow streets—are often blocked by buildings only a few feet away. Hanging a sheer curtain is the best solution to such a problematic view.

nearby chimneys bad feng shui. In China, people traditionally attach a small outward-facing mirror to any window that overlooks a chimney. This is said to reflect a chimney's bad chi back at the chimney before it gets a chance to enter the apartment.

A NEARBY APARTMENT BUILDING

Anything that hinders the entry of fresh air and sunlight is said to generate unhealthy chi. For this reason, any building—be it next-door or across the street—that severely blocks natural light and fresh air from your apartment is considered a negative influence. To blot out the offending building while still allowing sunlight to enter, install sheer curtains. Walls and furniture in light, warm colors mimic the look of a sunlit room and encourage the entry of good chi. To keep air from becoming stale, use a fan to encourage circulation and buy a few oxygen-boosting plants (just make sure that they do not need bright natural sunlight).

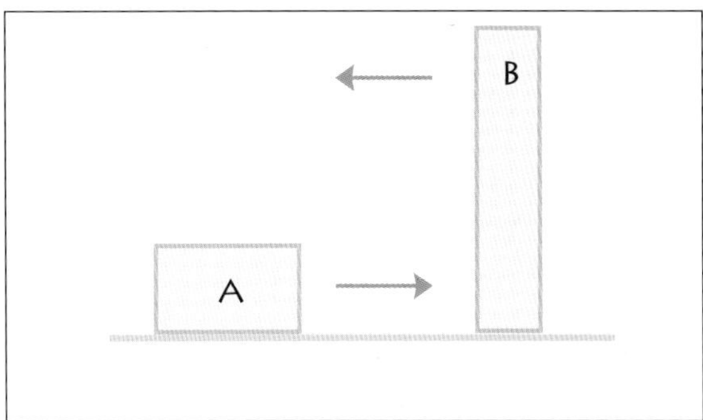

The view from building A is obliterated by building B, while building B's view is too expansive and needs to be narrowed.

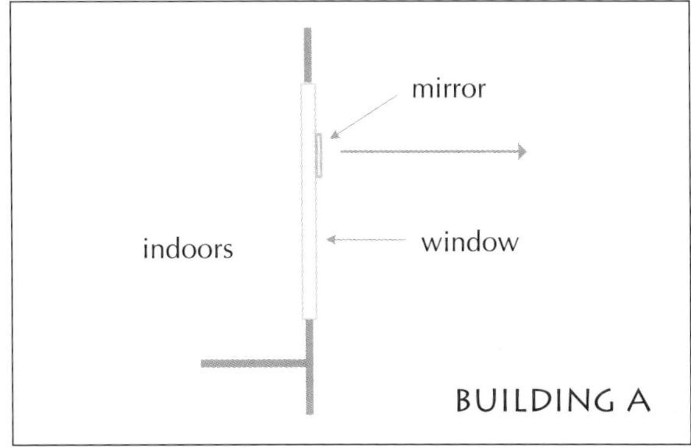

A large building that obliterates a smaller building's view is said to create bad chi. In the above example, building A can deflect the bad chi created by building B. How? By attaching a small mirror to the outside of the window—the mirror must face building B to deflect the chi back to its source.

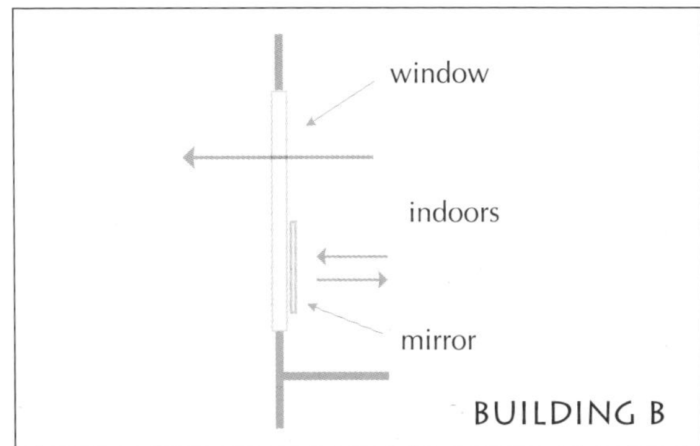

An overly expansive view is said to drain precious chi from an apartment or home out into the air. To reign in beneficial chi, building B can attach an inward-facing mirror to the inside of its window.

CASE STUDY
A REAL-LIFE APARTMENT

While many of the principles outlined in earlier chapters can also be applied to apartment units, an apartment's small space and compact floor plan does pose its own special feng shui challenges. To illustrate what some of these obstacles are, we present an average city apartment.

BEFORE

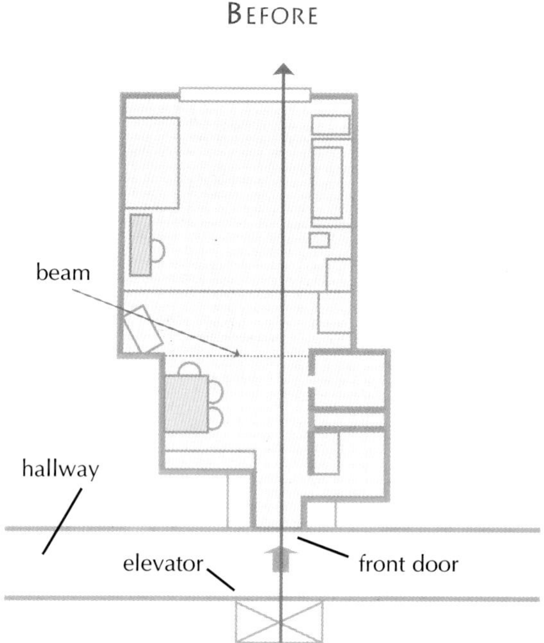

This apartment's biggest feng shui problem is the entrance. The elevator in the hallway directly faces the apartment's front door, creating a poison arrow or shar, which regularly hurls a strong jolt of negative energy at the apartment. To worsen matters, the front door directly faces the back window. In feng shui theory, a front door and facing window create a kind of wind tunnel that sucks any positive chi in the apartment from the front door to the window, where it exits. Thus the apartment's main problem is an influx of strong negative energy worsened by a quick departure of any positive energy.

Other problems that need to be remedied are a large wall-to-wall beam just inside the entryway. In feng shui, beams are said to constrict chi, affecting the occupant's finances and general luck. Also, a dark bedroom corner adds an element of negative chi to an apartment already bombarded with negative chi from the elevator's poison arrow. At its best, feng shui represents simple solutions to common everyday problems. For this apartment, several small, inexpensive remedies help repel negative chi while encouraging auspicious chi to linger in the apartment.

After

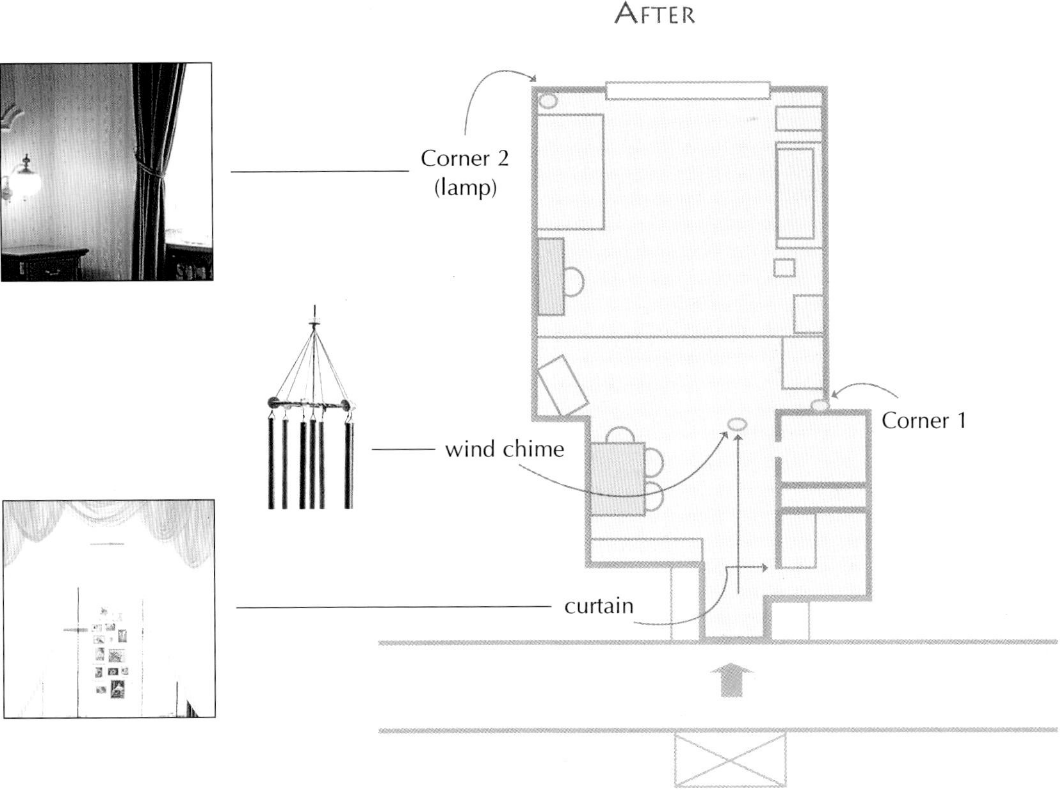

The most pressing and first area of feng shui business was creating an effective block for the elevator's poison arrow. A curtain was hung just inside the apartment's entry to block negative chi's entry into the apartment. To remedy the beam, two wind chimes were hung in two different places along its length. Wind chimes slow the travel of beneficial chi by encouraging it to rise upwards. This negates the beam's influence by bringing happiness and good luck to the household. Furthermore, the Chinese believe the tinkling noise a windchime makes symbolizes the movement of beneficial chi. To add light (which symbolizes positive chi) to the apartment's dark bedroom corner, a stylish reading lamp was placed near the bed.

CHAPTER SIX

FENG SHUI FOR GARDENS

THE CHINESE CONSIDER THE GARDEN TO BE AN EXTENSION OF LIVING SPACE; THEREFORE BALANCED, AUSPICIOUS ELEMENTS ARE IMPORTANT.

CHINESE GARDEN DESIGN

There is an old Chinese adage that says "a garden should offer a different view every three steps." Indeed, in feng shui, a garden's beauty is its most important quality—this is why the word garden in Chinese refers to an ornamental garden of flowers, decorative plants, sculptures, and ponds. Unlike North Americans and Europeans, who often plant kitchen gardens instead of decorative gardens—or who mix edible and ornamental plants in one plot—the Chinese do not like to mix what they call "food gardens" and "living gardens" (living space). The back yard is considered living space and as such, is cleverly designed with a balanced mix of plants, each in perfect proportion to the house's and garden's size. There are also a selection of carefully chosen stones, sculptures and water elements. No matter where in the garden you stand, the landscape will look different while remaining perfectly balanced.

What is perfectly balanced for one home owner, however, can seem unbalanced to another, leading feng shui masters to consider a garden's function before helping a client draw up a layout. Some individuals want a place they can communicate with nature; where they can eat, drink, and relax surrounded by plants and animals. For these people, plants that attract butterflies and birds are important, as are benches and tables that allow one to relax among his or her plants. A person who prefers to spend evenings in the garden would benefit from evening-flowering plants and discreet lighting. Others wish to pursue leisure activities, such as croquet or swimming, in their garden leading to the addition of a grass-covered clearing or a pool.

The size of a garden depends primarily on yard space and one's desire. Regardless of size, however, the fundamental theory is the same: bring nature into a home's living space and you will invite better energy into each resident's life.

There are numerous topics within garden design; in the following pages we discuss those elements most important in feng shui: plants, water, decks, stones, paths, and light.

A simple garden, even in a small urban space, can bring "smooth" energy into the household.

Instead of putting all of your patio furniture on the patio, try placing a few pieces in the corner of your garden to make a relaxing living area.

·elationship of the four major elements in a Classical Chinese garden—water, rock, plants and ·tecture—reflects the Taoist belief in balancing yin and yang.

PLANTS

In western cultures, mention the word "garden" and what springs to mind is a collection of plants. In China, plants are just one of several design elements used in a garden—however, they are a very important design element. When deciding on plants, the Chinese carefully consider a species' size, shape, and color. Feng shui practitioners encourage people to maintain a sense of proportion in their gardens. This encourages balanced, healthy chi, which in turn promotes balanced, healthy lives for the garden owners. In feng shui theory, proportion means that a clump of three-inch tall miniature pansies is out of place next to an outcropping of six-foot-tall bushes. Plants can be planted in containers or in the ground, as individual "showpieces," grouped in homogenous clumps, or arranged with plants of other types.

A garden that features plants with a variety of shapes and plants for all seasons attracts good chi throughout the year.

While a sense of proportion is necessary among fauna, feng shui theory also recommends cultivating a variety of plants in order to attract a variety of beneficial energy to the home. Thus, it is common in Chinese gardens to see plants with rounded leaves, narrow blades, or oval foliage; plants with a glossy sheen or a velvety finish; species that feature deep green, light green, and even red-toned leaves; plants that grow vertically, horizontally, or in rounded bushes; and evergreen, perennial, and annual plants. This last bit is especially important; as the Chinese believe that each season should feature at least one flowering plant. This means that a gardener must choose his or her plants accordingly. Even within a theme garden—such as a desert cactus garden or South African protea garden—such variety is possible.

This casual garden features a balanced mix of small, medium, and large plants as well as a variety of shapes.

If you are not blessed with a green thumb, or have little time to devote to an elaborate garden of hard-to-care-for plants, opt for a simple garden design featuring low maintenance flora—or hire a gardener to keep your specimens healthy. This is important because in feng shui, plants are powerful symbols of life and growth (physical, spiritual, and financial). To allow plants to sicken and die is to introduce sickness and death to your body, your spirit, or your finances.

This walled arbor is a cool, tranquil spot from which to enjoy the garden. Also, the ivy acts as an extra layer on the brick face, helping to regulate the temperature of the home's interior.

WATER

Water is a powerful symbol in feng shui, carrying energy that is nourishing, creative, and wealth-enhancing. Water is also a practical symbol, providing necessary sustenance for all life forms. For these reasons, feng shui theory recommends that homeowners who do not live near a body of water create their own. This sounds more difficult than it really is. A pre-made fountain qualifies as a body of water, as does a swimming pool, and a human-made pond.

Before designing your own "water body," think about shape. For example, although swimming pools are often rectangular, shapes with angles are considered harsh on the eyes and distract from water's life-supportive qualities. Rounded shapes such as circles, oblongs, and amoeba-like forms are best. Even better is a rounded configuration that gently embraces the home.

Those who do not have the resources for even a prefabricated garden fountain, take heart: You can still reap water's nourishing chi with a simple standing fountain—such as one of those plug-in varieties available at department stores and New Age boutiques—placed on the terrace.

Bodies of water such as ponds or swimming pools should be placed in proper position to the house: smaller pools are okay near the house, while larger ones should be kept further away.

Running water is most auspicious. If you are able to install a stream, try directing it under your deck to introduce active chi to the house. Carefully plan speed, shape, and direction.

Small fountains, such as this one, also bring auspicious chi to the garden and home.

An intimately sized lily pond combines both plant and water elements to provide positive, luck-enhancing energy.

DECKS

As the old Chinese adage goes, "where there is water, there is a *ge*." A ge is simply a roofed deck built off the back of the house. The ge is an important garden element within feng shui because it acts to bring nature and humans together—always a chi-boosting experience for humans—offering a place for people to congregate and enjoy views of their backyard fountain, pond, pool, or stream. In accordance with feng shui tenets, a ge is generally built in proportion to a home and garden.

From a feng shui standpoint, a roof is an essential part of a ge. This protective element acts as an umbrella, allowing users to sit outside during midday without being harmed by intense sunlight, or enjoy the sound of rain during a light shower without getting drenched. As we discussed on page 122, the Chinese consider gardens to be living spaces. Taoist scholars considered gardens to be tranquil sanctuaries for contemplation and inspiration. And as early humans needed shelter from the elements; a ge's roof provides shelter from sun and rain.

It is auspicious for a deck to be covered, which allows individuals to use the deck during many types of weather.

SMALL BRIDGES

True, bridges are traditionally associated with water. But you do not need a body of water in your backyard to benefit from a bridge: A small overpass can be used to transverse a rocky stretch of garden, a densely planted area of ground, or a small dip in the landscape—and in fact, in China bridges are commonly placed over these and many other landscape situations. Elevated structures bring a unique chi-enhancing element to garden design.

A bridge literally provide a "bridge" to help chi flow between different areas of a garden. However, different shapes, lengths, and widths can vary the speed and flow of chi—either enhancing or disrupting a garden's good energy.

Bridges help chi flow from different points in the garden, and their artistic forms help to balance the landscape. Natural substances such as smooth wood or polished stone are ideal.

However, there is one thing you should consider before building a bridge. As a bridge is also considered an energy element,. it should not point at the home or deck. To do so creates a "shar", which carries aggressive negative energy that causes nervousness and irritability.

STONES

In Western culture, stones are not often considered as a garden element. Yet, in feng shui, attractive stones of all sizes are commonly used to balance a garden's energy. Their shape, size, and location will affect the feng shui. In China, a favorite garden stone is called the Tai Lake stone, named after the lake in which it is found. These large, sculpture-like stones are often placed individually or in groups about the garden. According to the five element theory discussed on page 36, these stones contribute a solid earth element to the garden's large number of wood element representatives—plants represent wood. Having a variety of elements represented boosts and balances a garden's overall chi.

Their striking biomorphic shapes make Tai Lake stones a favorite Chinese garden stone. Outdoor sculpture can also be used as a feng shui focal energy point in the garden.

PATHS

If you want to build a chi-enhancing garden path, forget about efficiency. The most auspicious path is one that gently meanders, encouraging chi to take its time and touch those around it. Think curves, S shapes, and bends, and forget about straight lines. A straight path is like a straight river: it forces chi to move along quickly without spreading its auspiciousness to those nearby. This speedy chi is believed to cause edginess in people.

While there are no concrete rules on what kind of curves a path should take, feng shui masters generally agree on those elements found along a path. Plants and stones placed alongside the path should be chosen according to a path's size. For instance, tall, bushy plants can overwhelm a narrow footpath and strangle any beneficial chi traveling there; or a border of small violets can distract auspicious chi that is traveling on a four-foot-wide, gravel path.

Garden paths are treated like rivers and roads in feng shui: They provide smoother chi if they meander.

LIGHTING

Not everyone wants lights in their garden, nor does feng shui say that everyone must have lights in their garden. Who should have them: Individuals who use their gardens in the evening and early morning hours. For these people, lighting extends their garden's use, giving them a wider opportunity to enjoy it when they wish. To be "feng shui-correct," the size, shape, and location of garden lights should be carefully considered. Lights should be kept in proportion to plant size and limited to those places where they are most needed, whether that be lining a pathway, placed in the garden's corners, or highlighting a pool or fountain.

When choosing garden lights, opt for a size that is in proportion to the surrounding environment. This small light is ideal for a more petite garden.

COMEDY MOVIES
THE SMITH AND JONES WORLD ATLAS
TALKING PICTURES ★ Barry Norman
THE LAST LAUGH
LENNY BRUCE
FIJI ISLANDS
GCC TECHNOLOGIES
Macintosh Classic

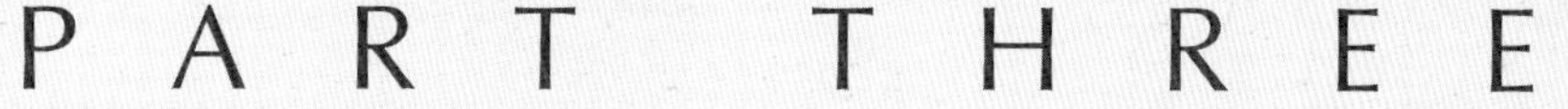

PART THREE

FENG SHUI AT WORK

CHAPTER SEVEN

FENG SHUI FOR BUSINESS

THE SAME PRINCIPLES THAT ALLOW FENG SHUI TO CREATE HEALTHY LIVING SPACES ALSO MAKE IT VALUABLE FOR THE WORK ENVIRONMENT.

UNIQUENESS OF BUSINESS FENG SHUI

Most individuals spend nearly half their lives working outside the home—a good incentive to make one's work space as nurturing as possible. However, business plays a different role in life than does a person's home, thus feng shui for the workplace addresses the unique challenges presented by business, including creating a vigorous wealth chi without compromising health-nourishing energy, acknowledging various employee personalities without compromising a company's needs, and maintaining success during slow business periods.

Before a would-be business owner decides on a business location, feng shui masters recommend that he or she pay close attention to timing. Within feng shui, timing refers both to the owner's personal life and the day of the month. In China, it is considered inauspicious to open a business when there is a serious illness in the family, immediately following a friend's or family member's death, when one is financially precarious, when an individual's marriage is unstable, or when one is in the midst of any other situation that weakens personal chi.

Timing also refers to the date. When creating a business, it is common for Chinese business people to consult something called the Yellow Calendar (see page 180) to help establish the precise month and day that should be the business's start date. The Yellow Calendar is a yearly calendar—available at many Chinese bookstores and stationary shops—that rates each day according to its auspiciousness. Remotely related to the American Farmer's Almanac, the Yellow Calendar helps determine the best days to start new businesses, plant crops, make money decisions, purchase homes, travel, and more. After an appropriate date is chosen, a business's construction and staffing is usually coordinated to finish in time for the designated opening day. (Note: The Yellow Calendar's accuracy must also be adjusted according to astronomical data.)

From location to building shape to floor plan, commercial buildings require a different approach than residential buildings.

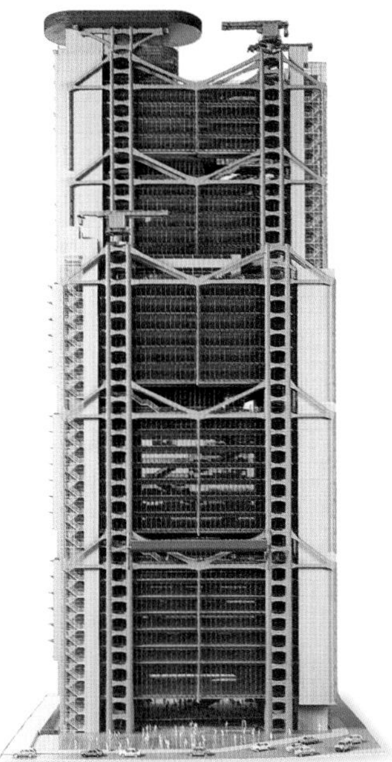

HSBC's former headquarters in Hong Kong, above, is one of the best examples of commercial feng shui application.

Busy traffic is beneficial for commercial buildings. The best urban planning separates residential and business districts.

BUSINESS LOCATION

Location, location, location. In western cultures, this adage underscores the enormous role location plays in a business's success—or failure. The Chinese, too, believe that location can make or break a business. The most obvious reason for a good location is visibility. When placed in a favorable location, a company becomes its own form of advertising. In other words, people pass the business, see it, and even if they do not enter they remember the company's name. When placed in a poor location, few people will walk past a business, meaning few people will enter the business or remember it.

But what, exactly, makes a location good? In China, a location is favorable if it is fosters auspicious chi. Among propitious sites are the following:

A corner location is ideal for business, say feng shui masters—common sense.

CORNER LOCATION

In feng shui, roads are treated as waterways. This means that a corner is considered "a spot where water gathers"—a good thing in feng shui, because it is a place that is continually fortified by fresh, strong, beneficial chi.

The active energy created by public transit benefits business.

NEAR A SUBWAY ENTRANCE

To Chinese, an underground train such as New York's subway, Paris's metro, or London's underground, is a symbol of the earth dragon, a lucky dragon that lives below ground. Any entrance leading to an underground train is considered a dragon mouth, a place where the underground dragon inhales and exhales chi. This highly auspicious location is believed to be rich in active energy, thus a business located on the same block or across the street from a subway entrance is believed to be very fortunate. However, feng shui experts do not suggest building a business directly above a subway entrance: the earth may vibrate slightly as underground trains pass through, upsetting an office's or store's chi and unnerving workers. Note that many feng shui masters also treat buses and bus stops as earth dragons and earth dragon mouths.

When choosing a business site, it also helps to be aware of poor locations. According to feng shui theory, the following locations are among the least favorable:

FACING AN ONCOMING ROAD

In feng shui theory, it is important to avoid shars. The most common shar associated with business is a road traveling towards a business's location. This usually occurs when a company sets up shop on the "T-bar side" of a T-style intersection, directly across from an oncoming street.

AT THE END OF A CUL-DE-SAC OR DEAD-END ROAD

Because it sits in the energy path of an oncoming road, a building placed at a cul-de-sac or dead end is also said to be poisoned by a shar (see above). Such a site traps the poison chi, where it stagnates, leading to high employee turnover, low worker morale, and financial instability.

NEXT TO A BRIDGE

A bridge encourages chi to travel rapidly from one spot to another. Because this chi travels too quickly to slow down and enter surrounding buildings, Chinese believe that businesses placed next to a bridge will die from a lack of chi. Note that there is debate among feng shui masters about businesses placed under a bridge. Some say that a business situated under a bridge will absorb a large amount of the chi passing overhead, while other feng shui masters believe a heavy object above a building creates oppressive energy that weakens business.

Feng shui experts suggest passing up office space next to a bridge, although smaller bridges can be less problematic.

NEXT TO, NEAR, OR FACING, A CHURCH, TEMPLE, SYNAGOGUE, OR MOSQUE

In many western cultures it is considered good luck to work within sight of a church. Not so in feng shui, which believes religious buildings create a strong spiritual energy that can overtake and strangle the active chi needed to nourish business.

FRONT DOOR

While the scope of this book is feng shui's Form School, theories from the Compass School can be used to give a business an extra boost. The easiest of these business aids is the five elements talked about in Chapter 2 (see page 36). To use, check the chart to the right for the element most closely representing your business. Once you have established what element your work corresponds with, you can use the chart to find what direction your business's front door should face. For instance, if your business is a fire element, your entrance should face south. A metal element business might get an extra boost from a west-facing door.

BUSINESS ELEMENT CHART

Element	Direction	Related business
Water	North	boat store/restoration, fishing, housekeeping, laundry, marine biology, surf shop, tourism, transportation
Earth	Northeast, Southwest	accounting, agriculture, finance, mining, real estate, tourism
Wood	East Southeast	architecture, carpentry, construction, education, law, publishing, stationary/office supply store, textiles
Fire	South	electrician, electrical engineering, fire station, food industry, lighting
Metal	West Northwest	auto repair, banking, jewelry machinist, martial arts

BUSINESS NAME

It is common sense: Your business's name directly affects its success. To ensure that a business name will attract auspicious chi and positive consumer attention, the Chinese avoid using inauspicious words in a business's name. In China, you would never find a chocolate shop named "Death by Chocolate," or a pub called "The Skull and Crossbones." Any word remotely related to death, illness, or violence is resolutely avoided, as the Chinese believe such terms burden a business with their negative chi.

BUSINESS-NAMING SUGGESTIONS

Evoke the business's purpose: A landscaping outfit should somehow make reference to landscaping. A shoestore's name should refer to shoes. While this may seem overly simplistic, the Chinese believe that a name that does not conjure images of the corresponding business confuses the public, creating muddled, weakened chi.

Easy to remember: If your town already sports three pizza places called "Famous Ray's," adding these two words to your own pizzeria's name will cause confusion among potential customers (creating weakened chi for you). A memorable business name must be somewhat different from your competitors' names. This is especially important in today's Internet climate, where thousands of web sites are competing to attract people.

Nice rhythm: Although sound is often overshadowed by feng shui's visual components, it is an important part of the philosophy. "Pleasant-sounding" is a subjective term; however, it is worth aiming for a name that is attractive-sounding to as many people as possible. From a feng shui standpoint, a frequently mentioned name helps business in two ways: Each time the name is said it infuses a business with chi, and subliminally, an oft-repeated name can lure customers to your business.

CHAPTER EIGHT

APPLICATION OF FENG SHUI FOR BUSINESS

RETAIL STORES, RESTAURANTS, CORPORATIONS, AND HOME OFFICES CAN ALL BENEFIT FROM THE IMPLEMENTATION OF FENG SHUI.

DRAGONS AND TIGERS

Groceries, auto parts, clothing, hardware, cosmetics, toys—you name the product and feng shui can help a store sell more of it while simultaneously enhancing a retail business's profitability, efficiency, and employee loyalty.

In Chapter 2 you read about dragon mountains and tiger mountains. According to feng shui, it is considered especially auspicious when dragon mountains are located to the west of a building, and tiger mountains to the east. Because the Chinese traditionally refer to the west as right, and the east as left—opposite from their placement on North American or European maps because south is placed on top—feng shui masters routinely use the lucky formula "tiger on the left, dragon on the right." For a retail business, the tiger represents the

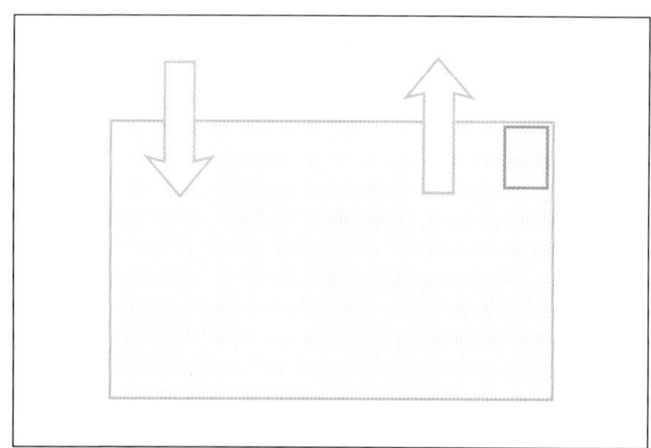

In China, it is considered very auspicious to place an entrance on a store's left and the exit on the right. Within feng shui theory this is called "enter by the tiger, exit by the dragon."

entrance and the dragon represents the exit. Locating the entrance on a store's left side and the exit on its right allows chi to enter the space, circulate, and leave when it grows tired.

ENTRANCES

The entrance door is one of a retail or restaurant business's most important considerations. It is this door that must keep out negative chi while allowing beneficial chi to enter. As in all other feng shui matters, proportion is imperative when creating an effective entrance. From the traditional Chinese perspective, the entrance is considered a business's mouth. An entrance that is too small will make the business starve to death, while one that is too large in proportion to the building will cause a business to eat up all the profits.

While it is important to keep the door in proportion to the building, feng shui masters suggest that for good luck, a business's entrance should be at least as large as that of the business across the street. Note that the key word here is entrance, not door. Within feng shui, one of the ways to increase an entrance's size is with an awning, which extends the entrance onto the sidewalk.

For many businesses, a small lobby or waiting area is an essential part of the entrance—especially for restaurants. Proportion and common sense are important to keep in mind when designing a waiting area. A buffet restaurant where people are up and moving around needs a smaller waiting area than a family-style sit-down restaurant where several parties may be waiting for a table to become available. A formal restaurant will need a smaller waiting area than a take-out shop where people must wait for their orders to be filled.

It is especially important for a restaurant entrance to be inviting to potential diners. As the fire element is associated with the food industry, this bold red entrance is a good choice.

ENTRANCE DON'TS

Try to avoid the following items in front of the business entrance:

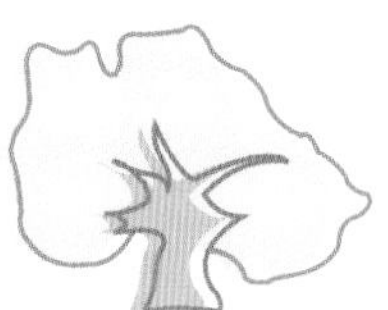

A tree opposite from an entrance. While trees are positive elements that symbolize growth, they are negative when placed directly across from an entrance. It is believed that they will block any beneficial chi that is trying to make its way into a store or restaurant. A tree that is taller than a business is considered especially inauspicious if it has branches that drape down onto the business's roof. From a feng shui standpoint, this symbolizes having weight on one's shoulders and is believed to lead to financial difficulties. Note that the smaller the tree, the less effect it has.

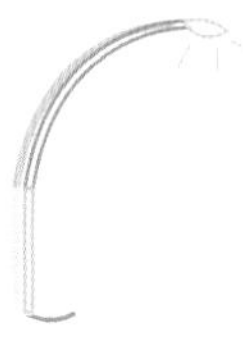

Street light across from an entrance. Like a tree, a street lamp that is situated directly across from a front door can block propitious chi from entering a store or restaurant.

A utility box placed against or in front of a business. In some cities, large light boxes are situated against neighborhood buildings. Feng shui practitioners feel that the large amount of electromagnetic energy controlled by such boxes can impair the smooth flow of beneficial chi in a store or restaurant. Note that the bigger the box, and the closer it is to a business's exterior wall, the more negative its impact.

Parking meter across from door. Like other objects placed across from an entrance, a parking meter is believed to hamper chi's smooth passage. In New York's Chinatown, one Taoist temple was bothered with a parking meter directly across from its front door. The monks' solution was to place baskets of apples or red ribbons in front of the meter to distract negative chi away from the entrance while attracting positive chi.

The space in front of a business's entrance should be kept clear to let positive energy flow smoothly inside. This outdoor mall, with its open clear walkway, illustrates the point.

WEALTH CORNER

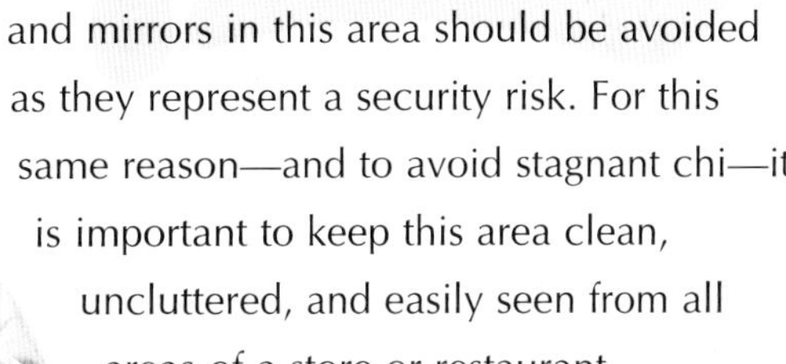

Though the concept is unfamiliar to most western business people, in China the wealth corner is among a business's greatest concerns. Also called the wealth sector or money sector, this is usually the southeastern corner of a business since in China the southeast is associated with wealth. To activate favorable energy in the wealth corner, Chinese business people decorate the area with symbols of prosperity, including coins or a painting of coins, a well-kept tank of healthy goldfish, or a desktop fountain. The light is kept as close to natural as possible—anything too dim will cause stagnant chi, while anything too bright will cause aggressive energy.

Cai Shen, God of Wealth

In a traditional Chinese business, this wealth corner would be diagonal from the entrance. This gives the wealth corner privacy, which in turn makes it easier to protect. For this reason, the cash register is most often placed in the wealth corner in most Chinese retail stores. Windows and mirrors in this area should be avoided as they represent a security risk. For this same reason—and to avoid stagnant chi—it is important to keep this area clean, uncluttered, and easily seen from all areas of a store or restaurant.

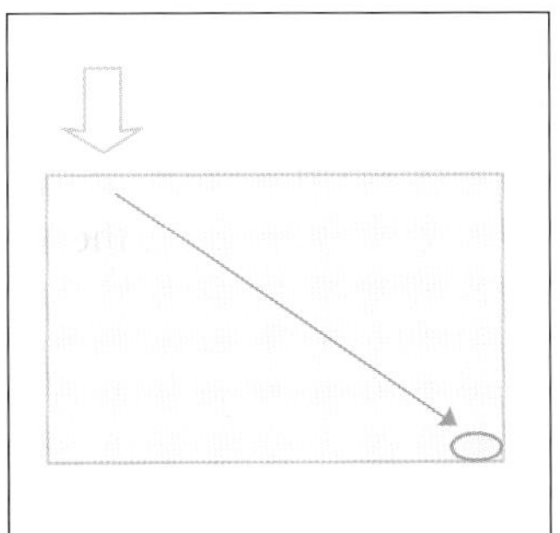

In a retail or food business, the wealth corner is most auspiciously situated at the corner diagonally across from the entrance.

When setting up a cash register it is important to place it at just the right height. According to feng shui theory, a cash register that is placed higher than waist-level will reject any wealth-enhancing chi that enters. A cash register placed below waist-level will loose control of any wealth-enhancing chi. One last note: avoid setting up the wealth corner under a beam, which in feng shui can harm financial success.

A healthy plant brings good chi to the wealth corner.

OFFICE BUSINESSES

Once upon a time office work was a rarity. Aside from a small number of individuals who worked in various financial, educational, or government positions, most people found employment as farmers, shopkeepers, blacksmiths, seamstresses, carpenters, and the like. But as the world's economy becomes more and more technology-driven, office jobs are no longer rare—they are the norm. To ensure both worker happiness and corporate stability, more and more North American and European companies are turning to feng shui.

Business feng shui usually requires a larger scale of energy management. This sculpture balances the huge plaza's energy.

MAIN ENTRANCE

A building's main entrance serves as a kind of gate, holding auspicious chi within a building, blocking the entrance of negative chi, shepherding stale energy out, and allowing fresh energy in. In general, the same feng shui principles that apply to residential entrances apply to office buildings: Doors should be in proportion to the overall building. Too small and they choke energy flow, creating a stagnant environment that may eventually lead to a company's death. Too large an entrance allows auspicious energy to seep out into the environment, causing a loss of profitability. In feng shui, revolving doors are considered especially beneficial: their steady rotating motion delivers a constant supply of fresh energy. If you are lucky enough to have the opportunity to design your company's office building, consider facing its main entrance south or southeast. In feng shui, these directions represent luck and wealth, respectively.

Revolving doors are auspicious for office buildings because their constant rotation supplies a continual supply of refreshed chi to the interior.

LOBBY

The lobby is an important element within business feng shui. It represents a building's "first impression" for incoming chi and incoming humans. Ideally, a lobby should be neither too large nor too small, but in perfect proportion with the building. An overly large lobby is like an outsized entrance: It leaks beneficial chi. A row of plants along the walls can help create a cozier, smaller-seeming space. A lobby that is too small creates a claustrophoic environment. This situation can be remedied by placing mirrors on the two walls that are perpendicular to the entrance door.

A solid, high wall behind reception acts like a protective mountain.

RECEPTION

While there are corporations that occupy an entire building, many companies own or rent one or more floors of an existing office building. For these companies, the reception area is vital in creating a beneficial environment.

The first thing a visitor encounters when getting off the elevator is a company's reception area. This area is also the first thing incoming chi encounters. To entice good chi to stick around, a reception area should be scrupulously clean, free from cutter and fussy decorating details, well-lit, and with good air circulation. The receptionist's desk should directly face the entrance and also be in sight of the elevator area, as the receptionist has to monitor the coming or going of individuals in the building (according to feng shui theory, bad chi is generated when a person cannot see who is coming and going). Also, a solid wall or screen behind the receptionist helps to protect his or her "back."

Keeping the reception area separate from the actual offices creates a feeling of privacy for office workers, while shielding them from the constant distraction of opening elevator or entrance doors.

BUSINESS BLOODSTREAMS

Stairways, elevators, and escalators are considered the "bloodstreams" of a business. The better and faster the access and service, the better it is for the business. Many office buildings in Hong Kong have their elevators directly connected to the street. The easy access allows for good energy flow.

The receptionist area here should be backed with screen.

OFFICES

Anyone who has worked in a company knows the competition there is for "good" offices. Typically, the higher a worker's status, the larger his or her office is, while the most low-status employees share offices or are assigned to cubicles. So what does this mean in terms of feng shui? That light-filled, airy, rectangular-shaped offices with windows may be the ideal, but most employees must make the best of what they are given.

INAUSPICIOUS SITUATIONS AND SOLUTIONS

DESK UNDER A BEAM

In feng shui, an exposed ceiling beam represents oppressive energy that can make a person feel depressed. Beams are also an obstacle to wealth, hindering a worker's ability to make money for a company. Hanging a windchime from the beam helps dissipate some of the negative energy while attracting positive chi.

WITH YOUR BACK FACING A WINDOW OR A MIRROR

In a small office it is common to see desks placed with the back of a chair against a window. This is considered inauspicious because it threatens an individual's security and can disrupt a person's chi. From a practical standpoint, a window can cause drafts, which can be uncomfortable on a person's back. Move the desk to another spot. Sitting with your back to a mirror is also unlucky.

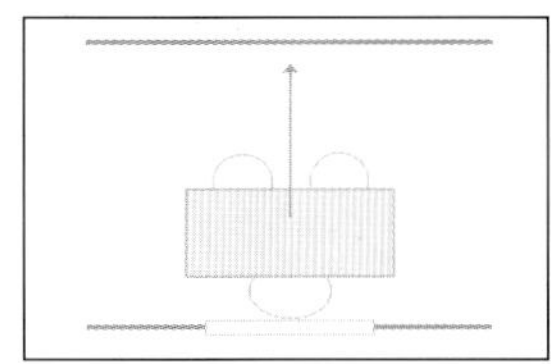

When sitting at a desk, your back should not face a window or mirror.

THE SOLE SOURCE OF LIGHT IS DIRECTLY ABOVE YOUR HEAD

Objects, like a light, that hang directly over the head, are said to put pressure on a person's head and shoulders. A better alternative is to place a lamp at least 2 feet in front of you, placed on the same side as your non-dominant hand. Situating a lamp on the same side as your writing hand can create a shadow across your work which feng shui experts say can dampen enthusiasm and motivation.

YOUR DESK IS IN A CONFERENCE ROOM OR OTHER COMMUNAL SPACE

A conference room or informal meeting room is a busy, noisy space that makes it difficult to focus on detailed work. If your employer can not move your desk to a quieter spot, wear earplugs to block out noise and ask for a screen or cubicle to be placed around your desk for a greater sense of privacy.

POSITIVE OFFICE LAYOUTS

A WALL TO "ANCHOR" THE DESK

A wall anchors a desk when the desk is positioned so the individual sitting there has his or her back to the wall. When situated this way, the desk enjoys high exposure to any auspicious chi in the room. At the same time, the wall is said to protect the a person by figuratively "watching his or her back."

DESK FACING A WINDOW

While you should not situate the edge of your desk directly against a window, it is beneficial to position it so you can look out.

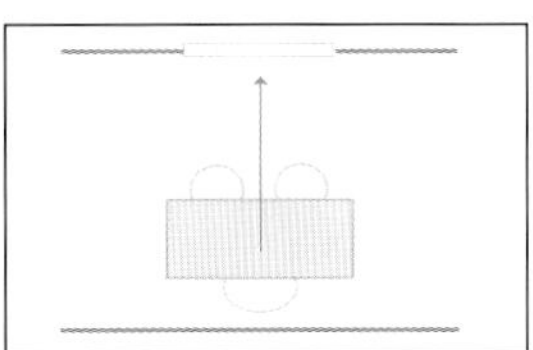

Ideally, a desk should be "anchored" by a wall and placed facing a window.

A HEALTHY PLANT IN THE SOUTHEAST

The southeast represents wealth in feng shui, while plants symbolize growth. Therefore, placing a plant in the southeast corner of your office helps stimulate money growth. Be sure, however, that the plant you choose is well-suited to your particular office's environment: a dead or sickly plant is a highly negative symbol in feng shui and can bring financial ruin.

KEEP IT CLEAN

Beneficial chi does not like messy, cluttered work spaces—so try to keep your desk neatly organized for good chi flow and better concentration.

Windows let in natural sunlight, which in feng shui is considered a form of highly auspicious chi.

POSITION OF CONFERENCE TABLE

When it comes to conference tables, seating can be a politically tricky business. Which side of the table is the head? If you put the president there do you put the vice president next to, or across, from the president? An easy and very effective way to position the conference table is using the Form School. The most prestigious position is the one facing the door, allowing the person seated here to see first anyone entering the room. This seat should have a support wall behind it. The vice president and any other important personnel can be placed to the president's left—or wherever they feel most comfortable.

Another, decidedly more complicated method of assigning seats is to use feng shui's Compass School. By researching the president and other company leader's ruling astrology charts, one can offer these individuals chairs located in their most auspicious positions.

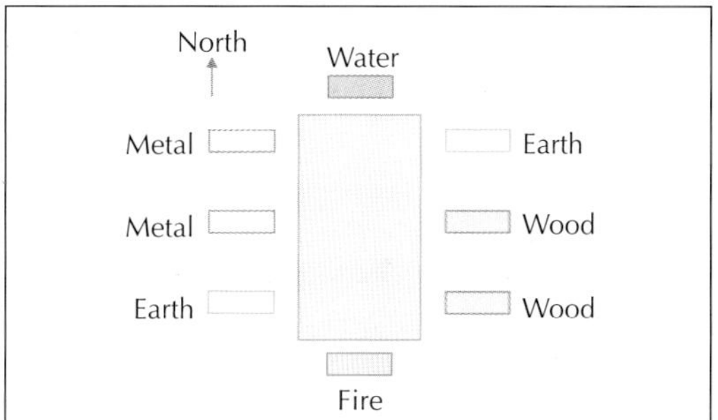

Above is a typical conference table seating plan—the most auspicious seat for each person at the table was derived from their birth element.

HOME OFFICE

Home offices represent a unique challenge within feng shui: How to create a productive work space without affecting a home or apartment's chi. While many applicable points were touched on in this chapter and in chapter 4 (see "Study" section on page 71), here we offer additional information.

Perhaps the most important piece of feng shui advice concerning home offices is "not in the bedroom!". Using a corner of the bedroom for work purposes is like combining oil and water—they do not mix. Each space needs a different type of energy—the office requires high-energy chi while the bedroom works best with calming, sleep-inducing chi. Mix the two and you may snooze while at your desk or ruminate on work issues while you are lying in bed.

Apartment dwellers who live in a studio or loft apartment will need to be creative in order to effectively divide offices and bedrooms. One option is to construct a wall, thus creating a separate office. A screen, curtain, or accordion-style sliding door are also good options. Or, move the office to a corner of the living room. From a chi standpoint, home offices do better when located in a common room than in a bedroom. Be sure to assign the office clearly delineated boundaries, otherwise officework might take over the living room, creating a cluttered, cramped look and inauspicious chi. As in the bedroom, a wall, screen, or curtain are helpful here.

This section of the living room also doubles as a waiting area to the office behind.

This home office is decorated in a mix of formal and casual styles. Its neat, uncluttered lines make it an ideal place for getting work done.

This home office in this apartment is not completely blocked off, but delineated by color, and the sculptural divider in the center. This kind of free-flowing design is very popular among owners or renters of large lofts..

CASE STUDY 1
RESTAURANT

This restaurant suffered from a poorly organized of its entrance and waiting area—two features that are especially important for restaurants, where people want their appetite and visual sense stimulated. There was not much yang energy in the building, and it needed more fire elements and yang factors to activate the auspicious energy.

BEFORE

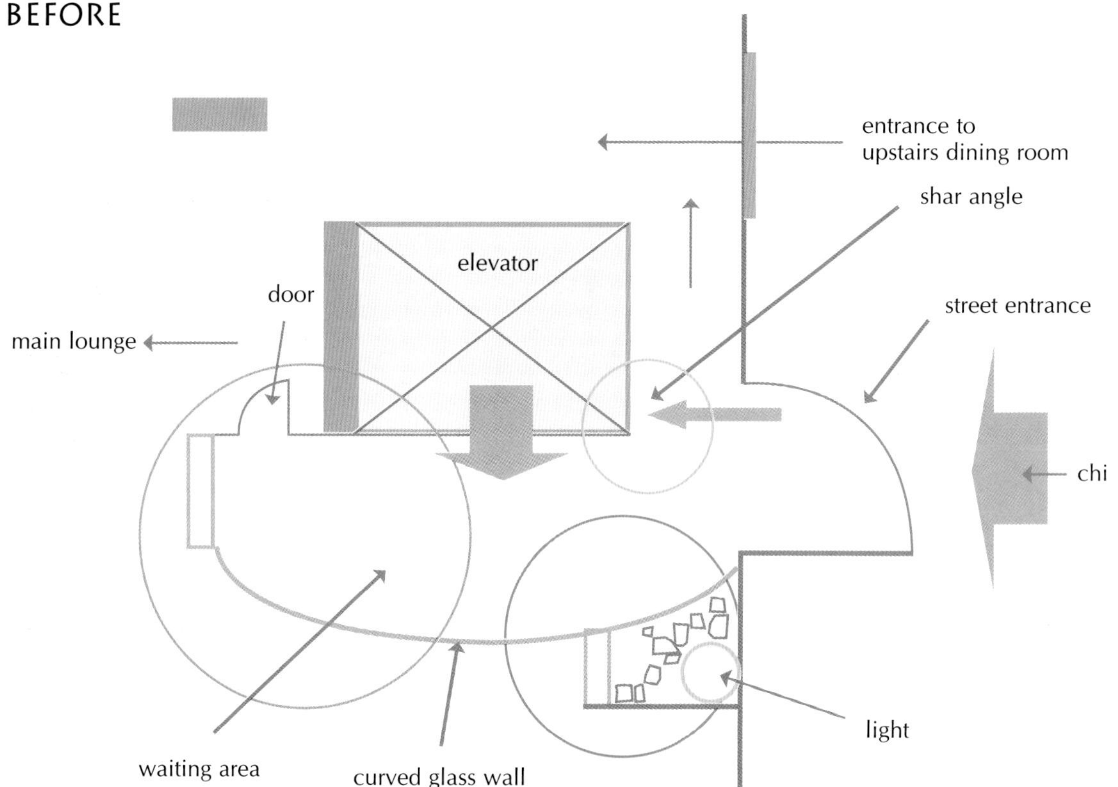

There is not enough yang energy in the location; the major problems are the stagnant energy flow in the three circled sections. Curved glass walls let chi escape. The building should have more fire elements and yang factors to activate the auspicious energy. Generally this can be done by adding bright color, more lighting, and adjusting the entrance to make it more spacious.

AFTER

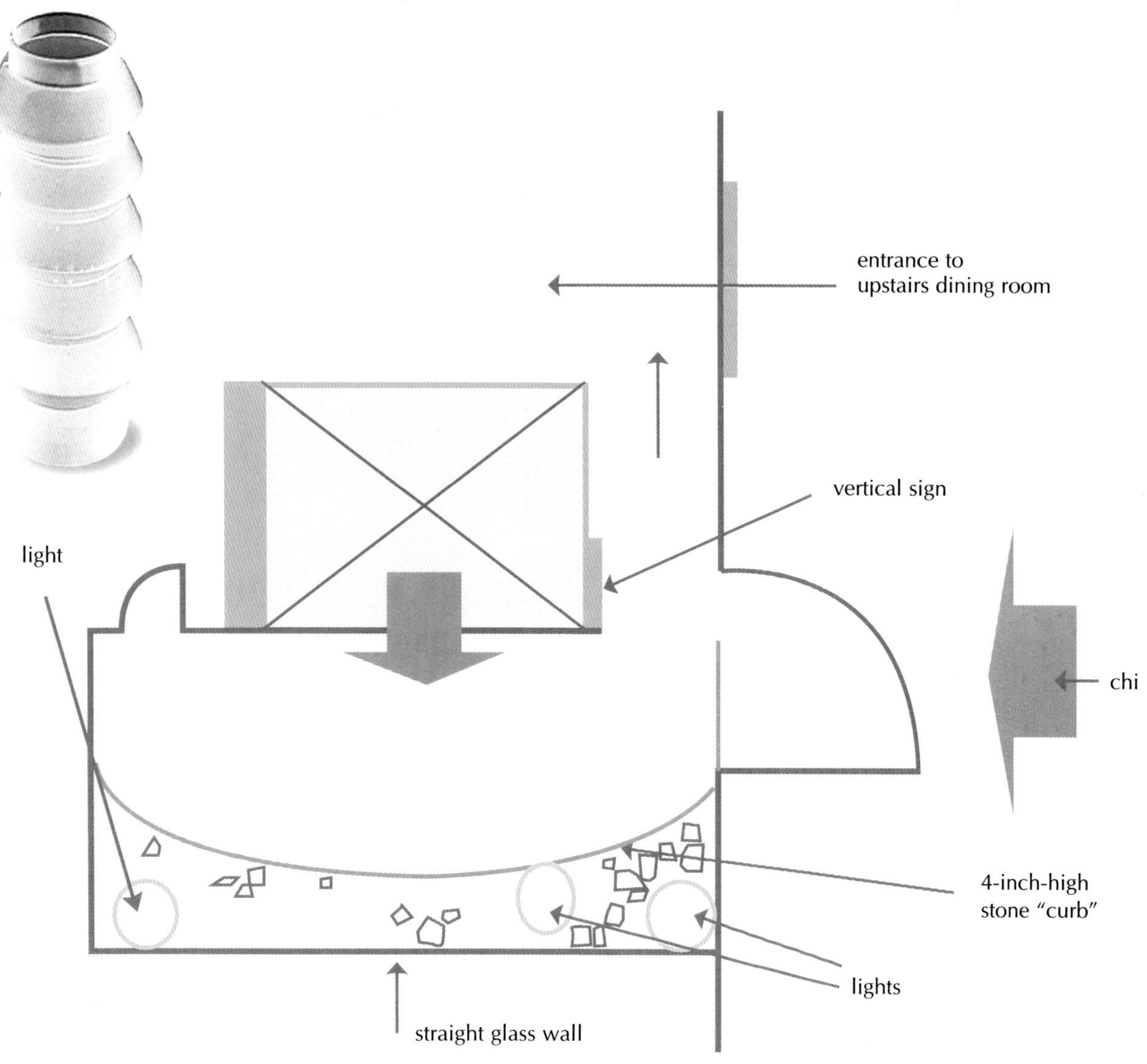

The entrance area was redesigned to let the energy flow more smoothly. The location of the lights was balanced with more items put near the entrance door. The glass wall moved to behind a 4-inch high stone curb that fronted a low rock bed to help the chi linger. More lamps were added—tall paper lamps in varying shades—to enliven the space.

CASE STUDY 2
COMBINED USAGE

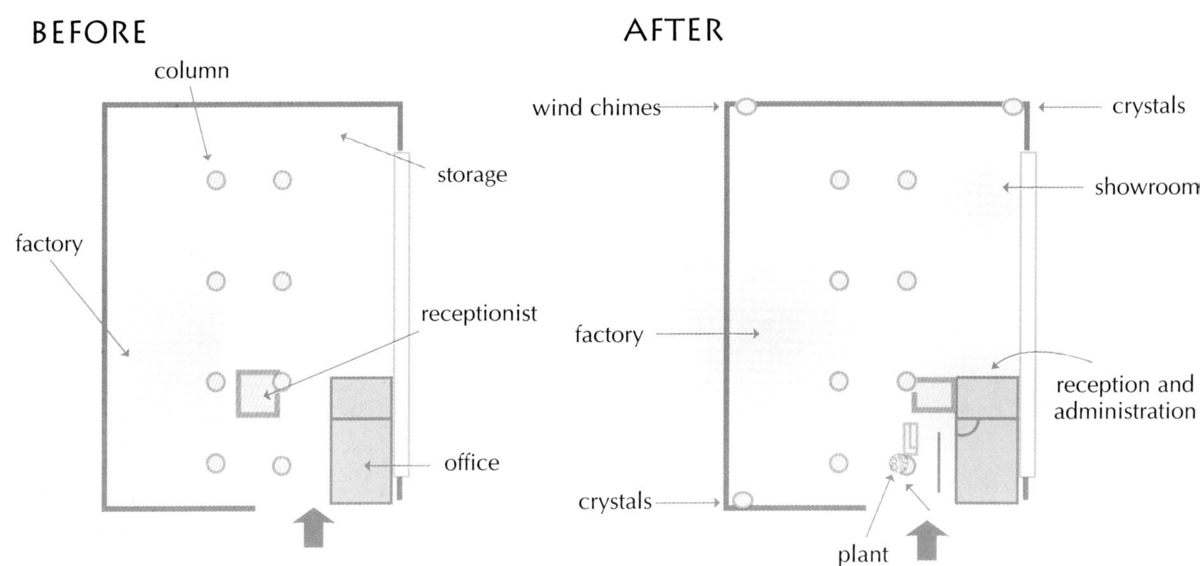

This space is unusual in that it combines an office for reception, an office for upper-level administrators, a factory, and storage facilities. Shown above, chi enters the space and rushes straight to the back of the building. The building's office space and factory—where the humans are—receive very little of this helpful chi. If allowed to continue this way, the layout could cause employee dissatisfaction and a high turnover rate. The exposed columns are considered especially bad chi and can impair wealth accumulation and cause headaches among employees.

This business requires many different types of chi. For instance, the factory chi should be more energetic and physical than the chi that enters the offices. To help energy nourish each of these areas separately, the space was split into clearly delineated reception, factory, office space, and public showroom. Notice the use of plants or lights on each column to neutralize the negative chi there. Other changes are a reposition of the front desk so the receptionist can clearly see the door, wind chimes and crystals hung in the space's corners to attract chi to every part of the space, and office doors that open inside (which helps keep good chi in the office while ushering additional positive energy from the outside).

CASE STUDY 3
OFFICE SPACE

BEFORE

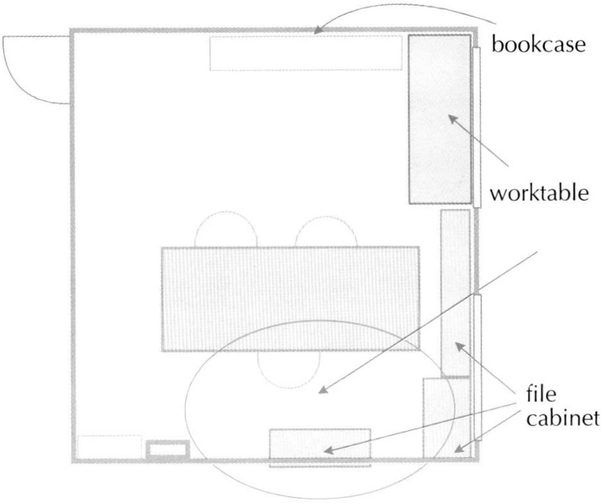

bookcase
worktable
file cabinet

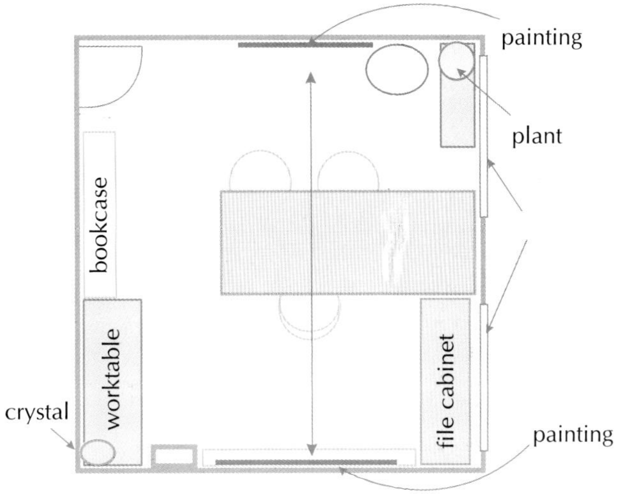

The main issue concerning this executive office is clutter control. Because the office has little workspace and little storage space, the president often uses her design table to hold paperwork, creating a messy, cramped appearance. A second concern is harsh afternoon sunlight which makes paperwork uncomfortable.

AFTER

painting
plant
bookcase
worktable
crystal
file cabinet
painting

Creating good chi can be as simple as moving a few pieces of furniture. Here, the desk was moved and the bookshelves and file cabinets placed within arm's reach—this makes officework convenient and helps eliminate clutter. Moving the design table to the left side gives the president more room to work. To soften harsh afternoon sunlight, see-through curtains were hung. A crystal was placed in one of the corners to encourage flow of chi, while a plant was situated in another corner tohold the energy inside as a guard. A large painting of a mountain was placed in the office to attract strong creative energy.

CASE STUDY 4
HOME OFFICE

The owner of this apartment felt that she was not making best use of it either as a living space or a working space. She worked on the dining table and the coffee table—resulting in papers scattered all over—and her bedroom was not relaxing as it was totally exposed.

BEFORE

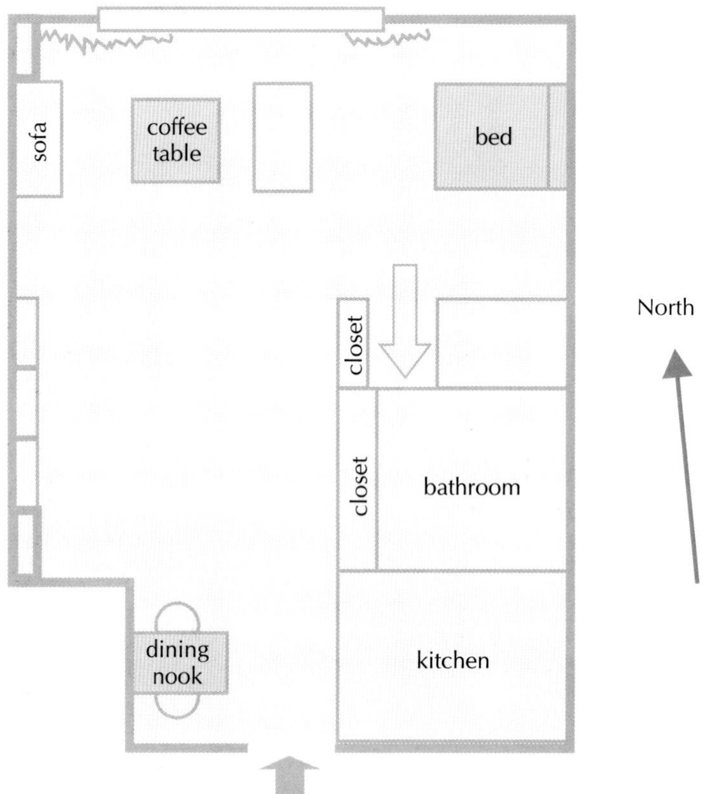

In many loft-style and studio apartments, it is common for one unbroken space to be used for sleeping, working, entertainment, and dining. Unfortunately, this "one room fits all" approach can cause problems. According to feng shui belief, sleeping in the space where you work can cause rest to be interrupted with thoughts of work, and eating where you work can lead to excess ive eating when one should be working.

AFTER

The first item of business was to section off a corner of the apartment to be used as a bedroom. In this type of situation, a wall can be built, a curtain hung or a screen installed. The entrance of the bathroom was changed away from its original position, to separate the energy into the bedroom and the bathroom. Because it helps to see the entrance while working, the office was located near the apartment's front door. To encourage energy to flow freely throughout the entire apartment, "energy activators" were placed in the corners. These include wooden sculptures, a crystal, and wind chimes.

FENG SHUI AND SCIENCE

OVER THE MILLENNIA, FENG SHUI, WHICH BEGAN AS A SCIENCE, HAS DEVELOPED ALONG WITH SCIENCES FROM METEOROLOGY TO BIOLOGY TO PHYSICS.

MAKING WEATHER WORK

Chi is the fundamental energy found in all things. For good health and peace of mind, this energy must circulate unimpeded throughout the body. Yet severe weather conditions can disrupt the constant, steady flow of this important energy within the body. Severe weather conditions affect the earth's magnetic and energy fields, which in turn disrupts the constant, steady flow of health-

supportive chi within the body. For this reason, one of the first steps in finding a home or business with good feng shui is to analyze an area's weather patterns. It is difficult to maintain good chi—and thus good feng shui—when individuals are distracted by uncomfortable heat, constant rain, forceful wind, or other strong weather. The following list is a general guide suggesting environments comfortable to most humans:

- **Temperature**: 49-75°F; 17-27°C
- **Humidity**: 30%-70%
- **Sun Light**: In China, it is believed that sunlight can kill bacteria—one of the reason's sunlight plays such a valued role in keeping a home healthy and fresh. Yet, too much sunlight impairs vision, creates glare, overheats a room, and saps moisture.
- **Wind**: 0.1- to 5 miles per hour
- **Rain**: A certain amount of rain is needed to maintain plant growth and water supplies for human use, however, the Chinese believe a region with near-daily rain can contribute to depression. In addition, copious rainfall can lead to flooding.

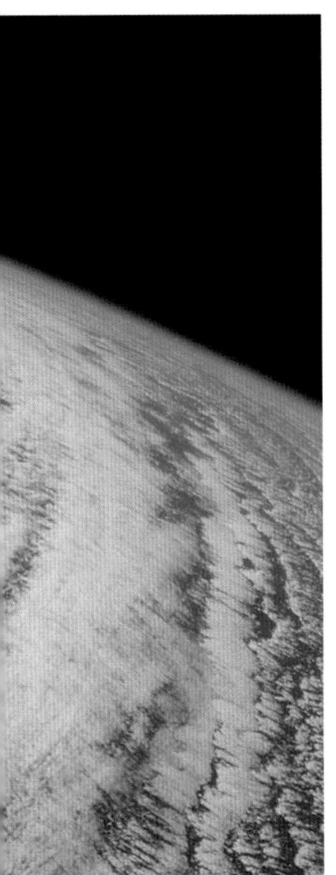

Weather has a great influence on human health. Both Chinese medicine and feng shui analyze weather as the first step in diagnosing illness.

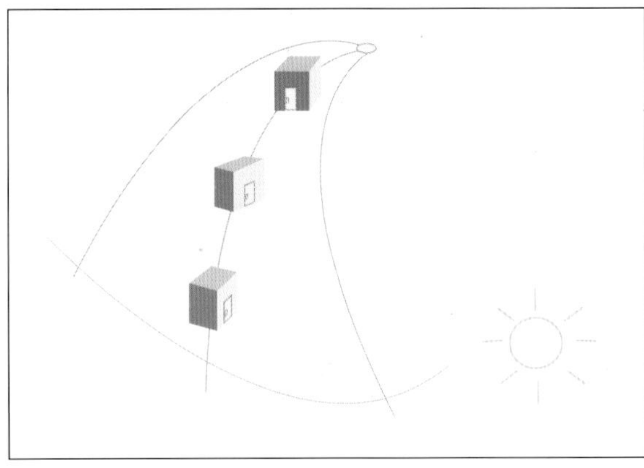

An area's proximity to the equator is one of the things taken into consideration when building a home. In feng shui, the further away from the equator a home is, the more sunlight it should access.

Early feng shui masters knew the importance of orienting homes and villages to take advantage of pleasant weather while simultaneously protecting humans from more severe elements. The most common way of doing this was to use a mountain or hill to block homes from winter wind. Furthermore, to keep houses cool in the summer, residences were located near a river or stream; the summer wind would travel across the water, growing cooler and more refreshing as it neared the dwellings.

Other weather considerations feng shui masters take into account: the origin of winter wind, the origin of summer wind, and the amount of daily sun available. Because of the vast differences in topography within various countries, the directions of these winds and the amount of sun a region gets may differ depending on the area of the country. After determining these factors, a feng shui master would suggest orienting a home in such a way that it (or at least its front door) is protected from the winter wind, receives a cool summer breeze, and allows in a comfortable amount of sun.

WEATHER AND HUMAN HEALTH

In China, it is believed that health is directly influenced by the weather. The following chart shows common weather conditions and their related ailments:

WEATHER FACTOR	HEALTH CONCERN
High temperatures	High blood pressure, heart conditions
High humidity	Joint conditions
Strong, hot, dry wind	Fatigue, malaise
Strong wind with humidity	Weakened heart
Strong, cold wind	Impaired immune system, general weakness
Rain	Colds, flu
Smoggy	Asthma, breathing difficulties

24 SEASONS

There are four seasons in a year, right? True, but many cultures—the Chinese included—break these seasons into micro-seasons. In China, these sub-seasons are known collectively as the 24 Seasons and are charted by a 24 Season Solar Calendar. This calendar is used much like the Farmer's Almanac is used in North America: to help farmers and other people who live off the land know when to prepare the soil, sow seeds, water fields, and harvest crops.

WESTERN MONTH	24 SEASON	NATURAL STATE
Early to mid-February	Li ch'un	Set up for spring planting
Mid to late February	Yu shui	Regular rain
Early to mid-March	Ching chih	Animals appear
Mid to late March	Ch'un fen	Spring Starts
Early to mid-April	Ch'ing ming	Green appears
Mid to late April	Ky ya	Good rain for crops
Early to mid-May	Li hsia	Set up for summer planting
Mid to late May	Hsiao man	First season plants appear
Early to mid-June	Mang chung	Harvest first season plants
Mid to late June	Hsia chih	Summer starts
Early to mid-July	Hsiao shu	Growing hotter
Mid to late July	Ta shu	Very hot
Early to mid-August	Li ch'iu	Set up for autumn planting
Mid to late August	Ch'u shu	Heat diminishing slightly
Early to mid-September	Pai lu	Nights cool off, dew appears
Mid to late September	Ch'iu fen	Autumn starts
Early to mid-October	Han lu	Getting cooler, more dew
Mid to late October	Shuangjiang	Frost starts
Early to mid-November	Li tung	Set up for winter planting
Mid to late November	Hsiao hsuch	Occasional light snow
Early to mid-December	Ta hsueh	Occasional heavy snow
Mid to late December	Tung chih	Winter starts
Early to mid-January	Hsiao han	Cold
Mid to late January	Ta han	Very cold

The 24 Seasons are often represented by the 24 vertebrae in the human spine, down to the lumbar region. To keep the vertebrae healthy, there are 24 different chi kung (qi gong) exercises, one prescribed for each of the 24 Seasons.

FENG SHUI AND MAGNETISM

Compasses, the tide, and weather patterns have one thing in common: they are each affected by magnetism. Think of the earth as an enormous bar magnet, surrounded by something called the magnetic field. Known as the magnetosphere, this magnetic field begins at the earth's core and extends far into space. Furthermore, the moon has a magnetic field, as does the sun, both of which play off the earth's magnetic field, creating the push and pull needed to generate tides, storms, the earth's rotation, and other natural phenomena.

Within feng shui's Compass School, individuals are seen as having their own magnetic fields, suggesting people should locate themselves in respect to their auspicious directions. This is the foundation of feng shui's East/West System.

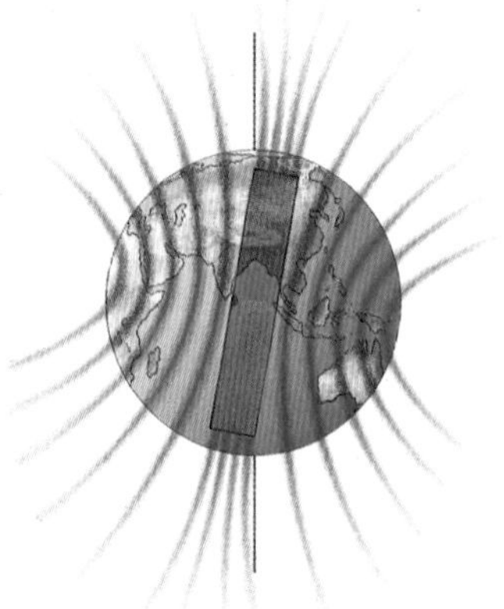

Due to the earth's rotation, distance from the sun, time of year, local weather patterns, and other factors, the magnetic field of any given location very slightly fluctuates.

MOON EXPERIENCE

While it is well-known that birds, bats, and some kinds of fish rely on the earth's magnetic field for navigation, magnetism's pull on humans is perhaps less apparent. Yet, according to the Chinese, humans have their own magnetic field—and are also affected by the magnetic field of the earth, sun, and moon. Chinese belief says that because the human body is largely water, the moon acts upon it in the same way it influences the ocean's tides. Therefore, full moons are often associated with changes in behavior—and with menstruation. In many ancient cultures, a woman's reproductive cycle was closely associated with the lunar calendar; in China, it is believed that menstruation coincides with a full moon. The Chinese term for menstruation is a moon experience.

Because we are almost 95 percent water, the moon affects us in the same way it affects the ocean's tides.

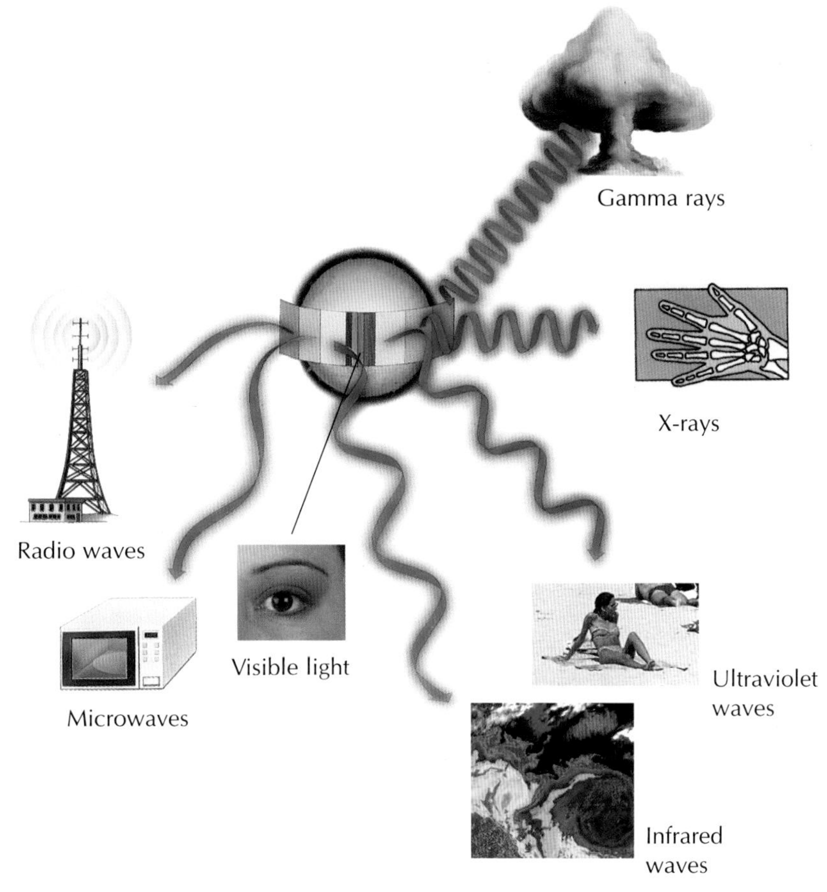

X-rays, ultraviolet light, visible light, radio frequency, and magnetic fields from electrical power systems are all sources of electromagnetic energy. These different sources are characterized by their frequency and wavelength--as the frequency rises the wavelength gets shorter. The nature of the effect of an electromagnetic source on human health depends on the frequency of the source. This chart illustrates wavelengths for various elements and objects we come in contact with in daily life. Feng shui recommends that you be aware of your surroundings, and limit interaction with higher frequency electromagnetic energy.

The earth's magnetic field flows slowly and constantly. It is a generally invisible force that does not harm humans. This is not the only kind of magnetic energy, however, that humans come in contact with.

Common sources of man-made magnetic energy include power lines, radios, electric clocks, computers, televisions, and microwave ovens. Though there is debate over how harmful these are to human health, feng shui practitioners recommend caution. For this reason, feng shui discourages computers, television sets, or other electronic devices near beds, sofas, and chairs. Here are some general placement guidelines to follow for good feng shui:

- **Computers**: At least 2 feet away from the bed. Also, when working at a computer, the chair should be positioned so an individual is no closer than 2 feet from the computer's screen.
- **TV**: Five feet away from the head of the beds, desks, sofas, and chairs, for a TV screen 19-inches or smaller; 6½ feet away for a screen between 20-inches and 39 inches; 8 feet away for a screen 40 inches or larger.
- **Radios, stereos, and electric clocks**: Two feet away from beds, desks, sofas, and chairs.

Keep in mind that elecectromagnetic energy is believed to have a stronger affect on infants, the elderly, or those who are frail, inactive, ill, or have damaged immune systems.

FENG SHUI AND CHEMISTRY

Many types of soil contain large percentages of iron mixed with other elements (such as calcium) as do some rocks, and human blood. This similarity in composition explains the Chinese view of earth and humans: The two are intimately connected. Like rich soil, a human body functions best when all the necessary chemical elements are supplied. A deficiency in even one element can affect a person's overall health mildly or severely. In China, a story is often told of a small town in which a large percentage of residents suffered from heart disease, something that is much less common in Asia than the United States. Upon investigation of possible causes, researchers discovered that the soil was deficient in selenium, a nutrient found in American studies to reduce the risk of heart disease and heart attacks.

ELEMENT	PROBLEM
Lack of calcium	Weak bones
Lack of iodine	Enlarged thyroid gland (goiter)
Lack of selenium	Heart disease
Lack of fluoride	Tooth irregularities

According to Chinese wisdom, chemical imbalances in the soil make for chemical imbalances in the body.

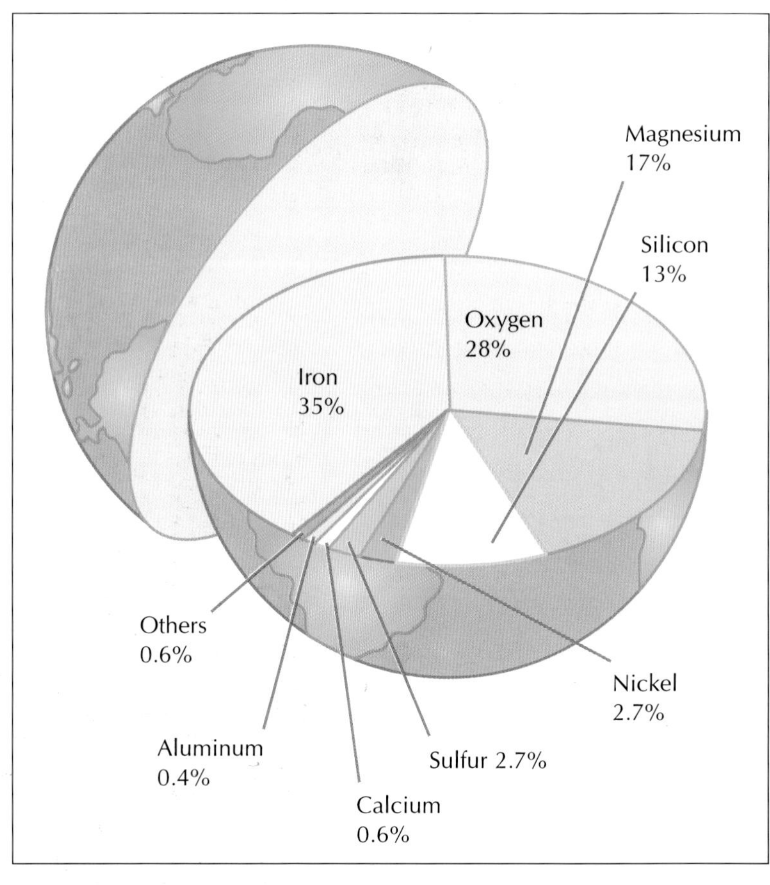

There is an almost endless variety of plants on earth; multitudes are fit for human consumption. Because fruits and vegetables are packed with all of the vitamins and minerals we require, the Chinese believed that humans were born from the soil.

As produce can be contaminated with pesticides or other chemicals, it is important to wash them carefully before eating.

Industrial chemicals are another type of environmental hazard that feng shui masters watch for. In many areas—urban, suburban, and rural—chemicals used in heavy industry, light industry, and agriculture, make their way into water supplies and soil, causing illnesses that range from allergies to skin conditions to cancer. This is why feng shui masters suggest studying an area's illness rates before moving there. An unusually high number of any type of illness could mean that something in the soil or water is not right.

Industrial waste can pollute the water supply and soil. If you live near an industrial center and want to grow your own vegetables, it is wise to have a soil test performed before planting..

FENG SHUI AND GEOLOGY

The placement of buildings, the shape of a river, the direction of a road, the elevation of a mountain—in China, all physical things are thought to radiate energy. Ancient Chinese were especially sensitive to natural landmarks, creating detailed rules for constructing homes, temples, tombs, and other buildings in spiritual harmony with their surroundings. If this harmony was achieved, then the spirits would look kindly on the family living there and descendants.

Soil, too, holds a revered place in feng shui theory. Indeed, fertile soil with an abundance of nutrients, good drainage, and a balance of sunlight and moisture, is the ideal for most of the world's peoples. If soil is not healthy, then an area will not be safe to live in and the ground will not be strong enough to support buildings. Like neolithic China, modern China believes that many regionally occurring illnesses are directly related to poor soil: anemia from iron-scarce soil; goiters, thyroid conditions, and enlarged necks from iodine-deficient soil; and heart conditions from selenium-poor soil. In addition, bacteria, viruses, and other microbes can reside in earth, causing illness among large populations.

To determine if soil was healthy, the Chinese tested it by digging up a shovelful, sifting it, and gently dropping it back onto the spot from which it was taken. If the soil had risen slightly by the next morning, it was a sign that the soil had good chi. If the soil had dropped and become level with the dirt around it, it was said to have negative chi. This soil testing was so important that early feng shui was called Kan Yu, or Survey Soil.

RADON

Radon is a naturally occurring gas produced when radium disintegrates. Highly radioactive, radon can cause low immunity to cancer. For this reason, it is important to test for underground radium deposits as well as radon gas, when building a home or other structure.

Feng shui teaches that it is not only important to find the ideal building location, such as at the base of a gently sloping mountain—fertile, healthy soil is equally essential.

FENG SHUI & GEOGRAPHY

If there is one principle most strongly associated with feng shui, it is geography. Feng shui's Form School is especially rooted in the study of a particular region's characteristics: its natural landmarks, weather patterns, benefits, and hazards. Originally, the discipline studied the placement of homes, villages, public buildings, and graves in relation to geographical factors, including mountains, vegetation, and bodies of water. These factors became fundamental guidelines for centuries of feng shui practitioners. Analyzing the relationship between local natural and human-made shapes allows a feng shui practitioner to orient a building to receive healthy chi. This also allows him or her to indicate auspicious building shapes, materials, colors, landscaping, and more. A region's geography also serves as a natural defense to protect an area from harsh weather and human invaders. For this reason, all China's early capitals were located well inland.

EARTHQUAKES

Areas such as Japan, Northern California, and Southern California are well-known for their active fault lines. Because these regions are frequently rocked by tremors and earthquakes, strict building codes have been created to ensure that structures will be able to withstand quakes. One solution is heavy metal support columns extending from beneath the building through the buildings upper floors. Another solution is balancing buildings on metal blocks which act as a buffer between the vibrating ground below and the structure above.

Plate shifting, volcanic activity, and other factors are all phenomena taken into account by Form School practitioners.

FENG SHUI AND BIOLOGY

Biology is the science of living organisms and vital processes. Feng shui, too, is concerned with living organisms. In fact, a region's plant and animal life continue to be important to feng shui masters on the lookout for an area with healthy chi. When studying the energy of a specific site, the ancient Chinese first considered an area's ground coverage. Whether comprised of grass, shrubs, moss, or other plants, the ideal ground covering was considered to be green and lush. Healthy ground covering indicated fertile, chi-rich soil; it helped prevent erosion of precious soil; and, because plants are believed to attract energy, ground covering helped boost an area's overall chi. Furthermore, a selection of hardy plants and trees indicated the environment was life-supportive, as did a large population of local birds, mammals, reptiles, and fish.

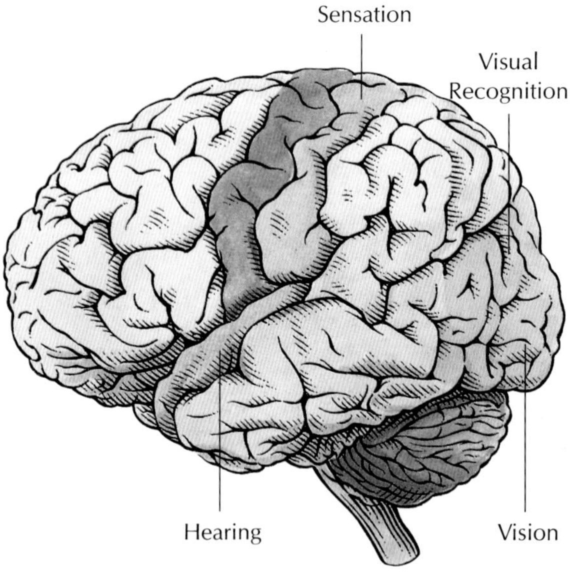

Feng shui is acutely aware of the power of the five senses—sight, hearing, taste, smell, and touch—as the basic tools that we use to communicate with the natural world.

Today, we humans seem less connected to nature than we once were, but biological evidence of our link with the earth remains. According to feng shui masters, the most obvious association between we humans and the natural world is our five senses. Sunlight continues to be a highly prized commodity among apartment hunters, home buyers, and vacationers. Natural noises, such as birds, ocean waves, or a bubbling brook, are more soothing than manmade noises, such as car horns, alarms, or car engines. Flowers, herbs, grass, and fresh air are more pleasing than many chemical fragrances, the smell of pollution, or stale air. Among the foods we taste, organically grown fruits, vegetables, and grains represent less of a health hazard than pre-packaged convenience foods made with fake colorings, artificial flavorings, and chemical preservatives. Studies have shown that stroking an animal's fur lowers human blood pressure, which partially explains the human love of soft, tactile fabrics, and decorating materials over manmade synthetic materials.

DEALING WITH NOISE AND AIR POLLUTION

As we humans rely less and less on the land for survival, we are faced with more and more pollution. Air pollution and noise pollution are an established part of modern life and must be considered when creating a healthy living or working environment.

Excess noise has been linked to increases in blood pressure, stress, and anxiety, while polluted air can contribute to red eyes, asthma, allergies, pulmonary conditions, and cancer. Therefore, structures built in noisy neighborhoods, or in areas with unclean air, require greater protection from the outdoors. Protective measures include building with wood instead of stucco or brick (wood absorbs sound better) and installing double-glass windows, tight-fitting seals around windows and doors, ceiling fans for indoor air circulation, and perhaps even a home air filter.

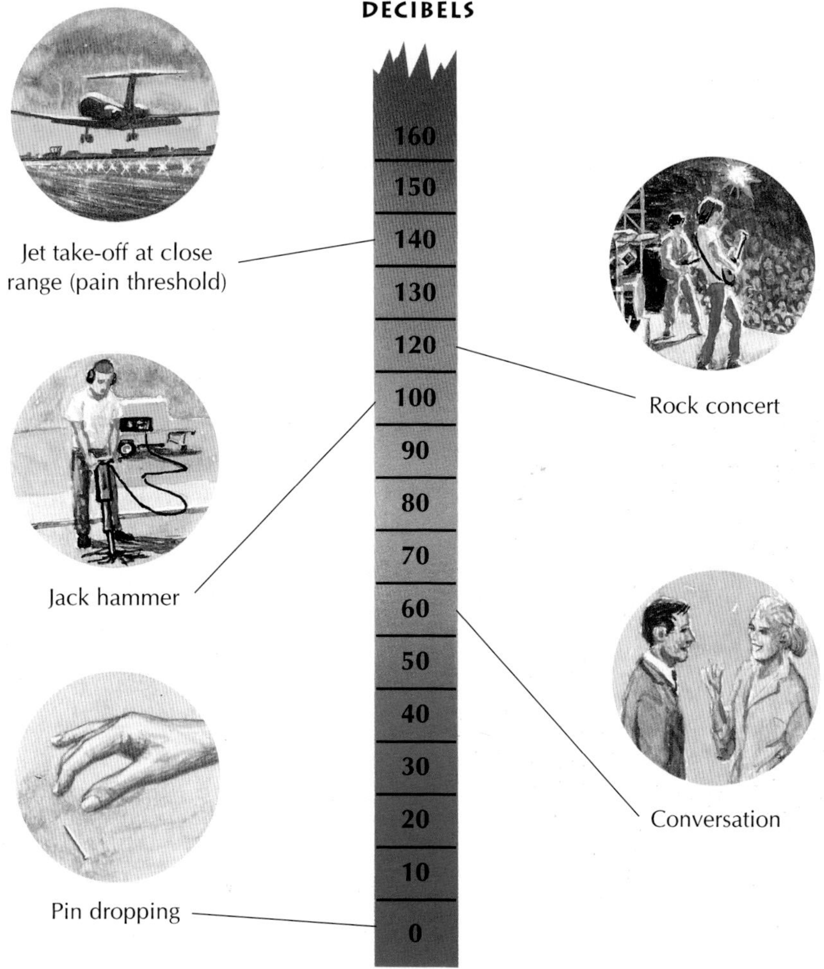

This chart illustrates the intensity level of sound, or decibels, for common sounds we may hear. Sounds of 140 decibels or more can damage hearing, but even 60 to 70 decibels can cause stress if repetitive.

THE FENG SHUI-CHINESE MEDICINE CONNECTION

Thanks to their common Taoist ancestry, feng shui and Chinese medicine have several things in common, including their use of chi, yin and yang, and the five elements. However, perhaps their greatest similarity is their use of balance (either in a physical space or in the body) to create human well-being.

While neolithic Chinese shamans were well-versed in the use of herbal medicine and energy work, Chinese medicine was officially born with the appearance of *The Yellow Emperor's Classic of Medicine*, more than 5000 years ago. One of the best-known and earliest Chinese medical texts, many believe it was written during the third millennium BC by the mythical Yellow Emperor. Besides general theory, the book discusses natural drugs, gymnastics, and minor surgery.

Many of the concepts presented in the *Classic of Medicine* have become well-established elements of modern Chinese medicine. The most central of these is the maintenance of balance. Ideally, the human body should be in a perfectly equalized state. Activity should match rest, intake of food

EXCERPTS FROM THE YELLOW EMPORER'S CLASSIC OF MEDICINE

"Nature has four seasons and five elements. To grant long life, these seasons and elements must store up the power of creation in cold, heat, dryness, moisture, and wind. Man has five viscera in which these five climates are transformed into joy, anger, sympathy, grief. and fear. The emotions of joy and anger are injurious to the spirit just as cold and heat are injurious to the body. Violent anger depletes Yin; violent joy depletes Yang. When rebellious emotions rise to Heaven, the pulse expires and leaves the body. When joy and anger are without moderation, then cold and heat exceed all measure, and life is no longer secure. Yin and Yang should be respected to an equal extent."

By using feng shui to improve one's surroundings and Chinese medicine to maintain health, the Chinese believe that one can live a long, healthy life like Tao Te Chang, God of Longevity.

should match outflow of calories and so on. This is important because illness is caused by an imbalance of yin and yang due to intense emotions, activity, temperature, or other influences. Curing an illness thus depends on accurately finding the source of the imbalance. Because the body's organs and systems are interrelated, diagnosing an imbalance can be tricky. For example, the liver is considered a yin organ because it is solid. But the liver is thought to promote the flow of energy, which is a yang quality.

Acupuncture, herbal treatments, chi kung, sexual harnessing of yin and yang—all are health-supportive measures used within Chinese medicine to maintain or create a balance between yin and yang. After all, in both feng shui and Chinese medicine, when yin and yang are brought into balance, illness is diminished and well-being and vitality are increased.

Checking the pulse, looking at the face, listening to the voice, and asking diagnostic questions are the four basic methods in traditional Chinese medical practice.

TYPES OF IMBALANCE

Perhaps nowhere is the concept of yin and yang so well-known to Westerners as in Chinese medicine. There are many types of imbalances between yin and yang. When trying to decide what type of disparity is present, doctors of Chinese medicine look for the following clues:

- **Too much Yin**: Characterized by cold symptoms, including joint problems, bone conditions, and kidney disorders.
- **Too much Yang**: Characterized by heat symptoms, including circulation conditions, heart problems, and fevers.
- **Too little Yin**: Characterized by internal heat symptoms, including skin conditions, and lowered ability to tolerate physical or emotional stress.
- **Too little Yang**: Characterized by general coldness, including fatigue, general weakness, and incontinence.

The Taoist philosophy of balance among humans, Earth, and the universe are central to feng shui and Chinese medicine

YIN & YANG FOODS

At the beginning of Chinese civilization, people ate whatever the Earth offered with no thought given to what may be poisonous. Soon, people grew sick—some even died. Upon learning this, the mythical Shen Nong Shi (Holy Farmer Fellow) began teaching people how to forage for and grow nonpoisonous plants. Around this time, the Chinese defined 100 plants that could be used as food, 100 plants that could be used as medicine, and 100 plants that could be used both as food and medicine. (For example, hawthorn fruit is used in China as food and as a heart medicine, while Chinese dates are both a popular snack and a treatment for boosting red blood cell counts.) The same categories are still being used today in Chinese medicine.

The Chinese continue to believe that food is a more effective medicine than human-made drugs. Unlike drugs, which treat a specific body condition medicine (and in turn can lead to separate health conditions), healing foods address both the condition and the body with more success, fewer side effects, and less overall damage to the patient.

YIN FOODS

juice greens melon dairy products tea

As a general rule, the Chinese categorize foods as either yin or yang. Yin foods are eaten to balance yang conditions within the body or surrounding environment, while yang foods are eaten to balance yin conditions within the body or surrounding environment.

Yin foods: melons, green vegetables, leafy vegetables, fruit juice, dairy products, watery foods, green tea

Yang foods: bananas, nuts, seeds, legumes, oils, fatty or rich foods, black tea, pungent spices, chocolate, coffee

YANG FOODS

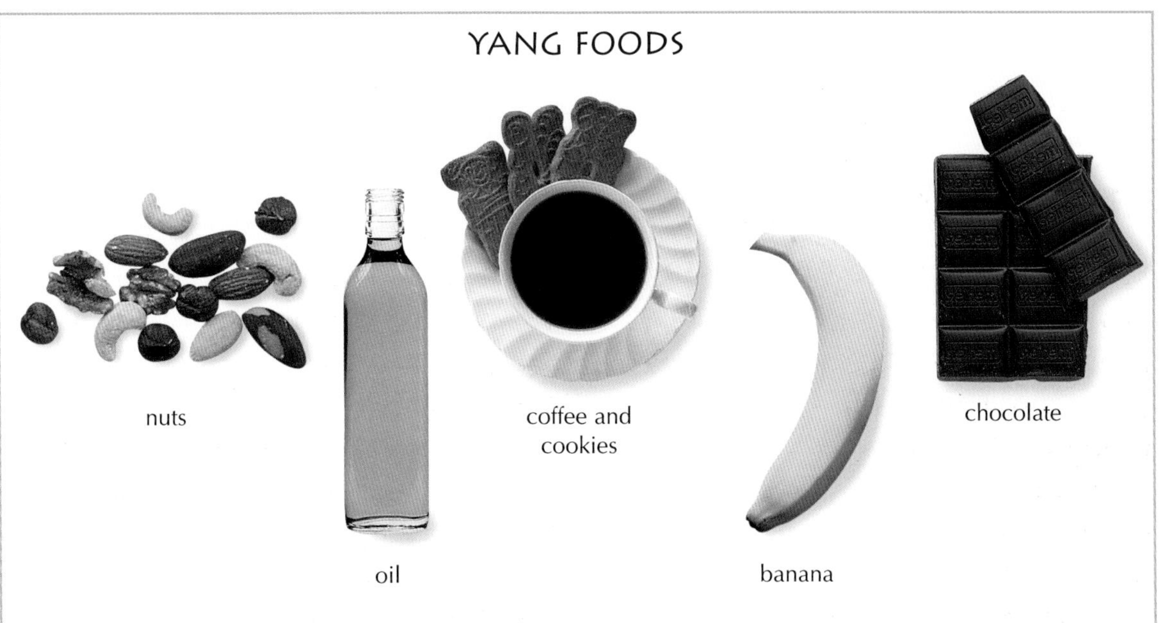

HERBS

wolfberry

ginseng

Not only do the Chinese categorize different foods as yin or yang, the Chinese also believe that certain herbs possess yin or yang qualities as well. Yin herbs such as wolfberry help to improve yin energy, while ginseng is a well-known yang-energy booster.

THE FIVE ELEMENTS

While yin and yang may be the pillar of Chinese medicine, the five elements (also called the five phases) established by the Yellow Emperor also play a role when diagnosing and treating diseases. The following conditions occur when too much of one element is present in a person's body or surroundings.

ELEMENT	POSSIBLE CONDITIONS
Fire	Headaches, fever, incoherence, disease of one of the inner organs
Water	Kidney disease, nausea, vomiting, diarrhea, parasites
Metal	Coughs, asthma, general weakness, fatigue, unexplained weight loss, bone aches
Wood	Stiff muscles and joints, liver disease, jaundice, sallow skin, stroke, nerve system condition, facial paralysis
Earth	Stomach aches, digestive upset, rashes, influenza

ACUPUNCTURE

To the uninitiated, getting pricked with needles may seem a strange way to foster health and well-being, but in China people have been doing just that—with impressive results—for over 5000 years. Called acupuncture, the practice was born when the Yellow Emperor's book described something called meridians. Because chi circulates in the body along these energy pathways, these meridians were said to be the central pathways for a human's life, death, health, illness, and emotions. There are 12 of these meridians, each linked to specific internal organs and organ systems. Furthermore, there are over 1000 spots along the meridian system that can be stimulated to enhance the flow of chi. These are called accupoints, and when special needles (sterilized or disposable, stainless steel, and hair-thin) are inserted into them the flow of chi is corrected and rebalanced. When chi flow is good, so is one's health.

Interestingly, Western research has validated the existence of these meridians. One of the best-known studies was conducted in the 1970s. Under a grant from the National Institutes of Health, Robert O Becker, M.D., and Maria Reichmanis, a biophysicist, found that electrical currents did indeed flow along the ancient Chinese meridians . They also discovered that the acupuncture points–at least 25 percent of them–did exist along those scientifically measurable lines. Explaining acupuncture's success, they theorized that

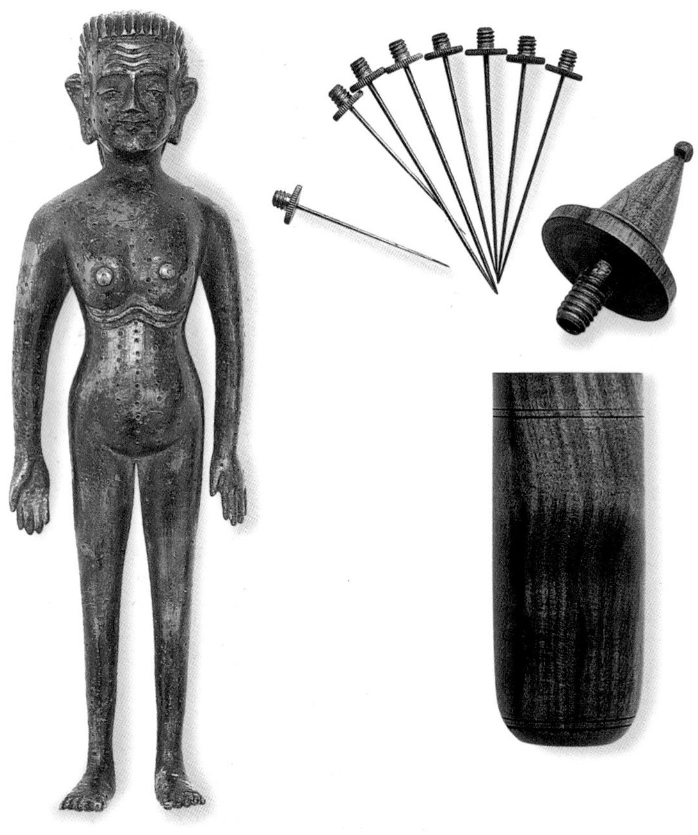

Chinese acupuncture was developed according to a chi meridian system of the human body. We each have 12 meridians.

inserting needles along accupoints could alter energy flow and thus block pain stimulus. More recent research has found that acupuncture stimulates the body to release natural painkillers called endorphins and enkephalins, as well as anti-inflammatory agents called cortisol.

Like feng shui, acupuncture was developed by early Taoists. This explains the similarities between the two: the focus on chi, the need for free-flowing energy, the importance of balance, and the diagnostic use of yin and yang, the five elements, and the pa kua.

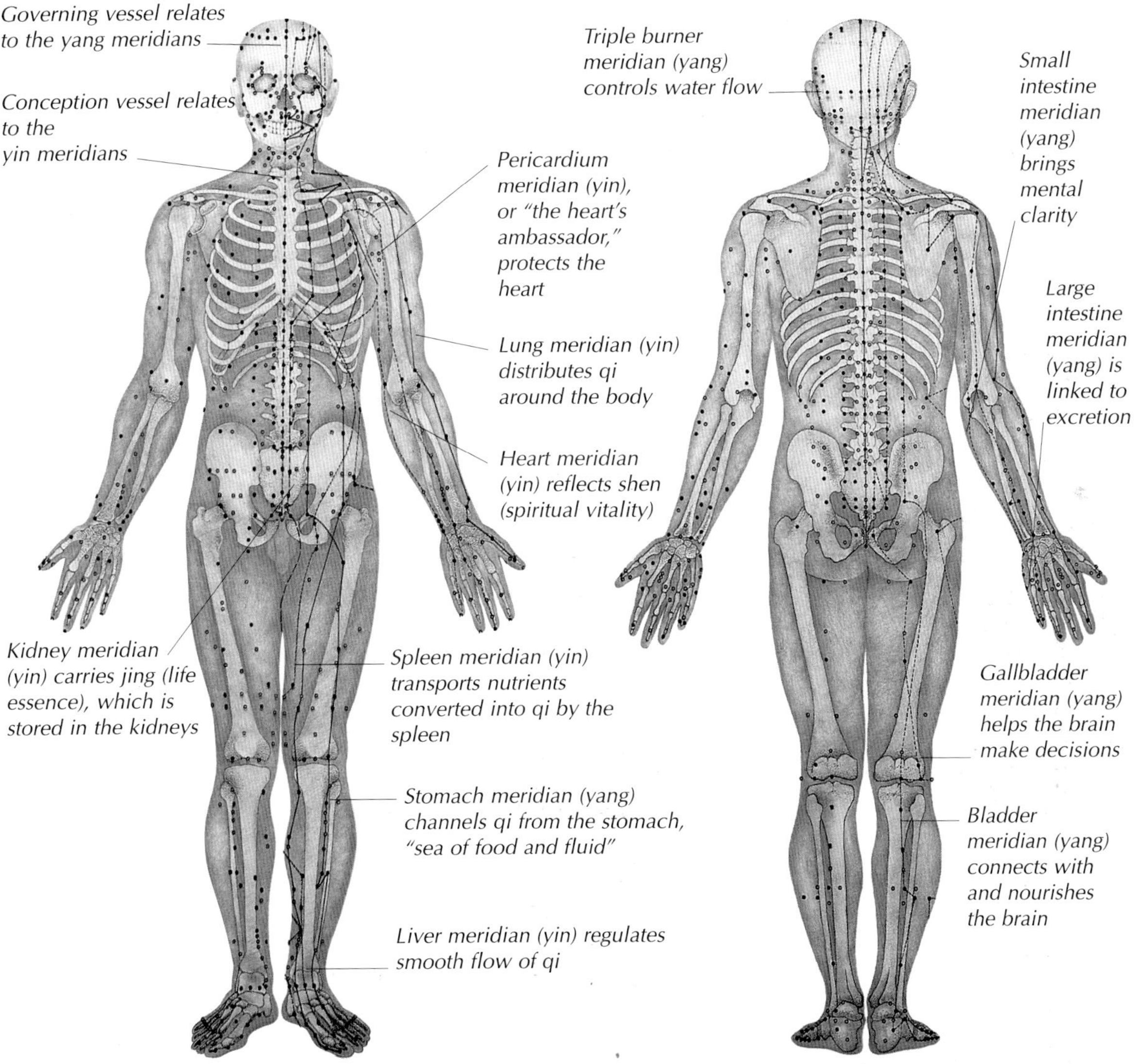

Each meridian links to a specific organ, which can be rebalanced by stimulation of one or more of the over 1,000 spots along the system called acupoints. As feng shui manages chi outside of the body, acupuncture directs the flow of chi within. In their evaluations, feng shui masters factor in the chi flow, or health of the person or persons who will be occupying the living or working space, and plan accordingly.

CALENDARS AND CHRONOLOGIES

THE TRADITIONAL CHINESE CALENDAR COMBINES BOTH LUNAR AND SLOAR ASPECTS AND DOES NOT EXACTLY MATCH THE WESTERN CALENDAR

CHINESE CALENDAR

Unlike the solar Gregorian calendar used by Western cultures, the traditional Chinese calendar combines both lunar and solar dates. The individual years are the same in both Western Gregorian and modern Chinese solar calendars, where the solar calendar starts on either the 4th or 5th of February, mid-way between the Winter Solstice and Spring Equinox.

Instead of starting in January the Chinese lunar New Year can start anywhere from late January to mid-February depending on the year.

NOTE: To determine your Chinese astrology sign, simply find the Chinese lunar year of your birth on page 173 and turn to page 174 to read your astrological animal's personality profile. Individuals born in January or the start of February need to pay special attention to when each Chinese lunar year begins.

CHINESE YEAR	GREGORIAN CALENDAR DATES	ELEMENT	ANIMAL SIGN	CHINESE YEAR	GREGORIAN CALENDAR DATES	ELEMENT	ANIMAL SIGN
1924	Feb. 5, 1924–Jan. 24, 1925	wood	rat	1965	Feb. 2, 1965–Jan. 20, 1966	wood	snake
1925	Jan. 25, 1925–Feb. 12, 1926	wood	ox	1966	Jan 21, 1966–Feb. 8, 1967	fire	horse
1926	Feb. 13, 1926–Feb. 1, 1927	fire	tiger	1967	Feb. 9, 1967–Jan. 29, 1968	fire	goat
1927	Feb. 2 1927–Jan. 22 1928	fire	rabbit	1968	Jan. 30, 1968–Feb. 16, 1969	earth	monkey
1928	Jan. 23, 1928–Feb. 9, 1929	earth	dragon	1969	Feb. 17, 1969–Feb. 5, 1970	earth	rooster
1929	Feb. 10, 1929–Jan. 30, 1930	earth	snake	1970	Feb. 6, 1970–Jan. 26, 1971	metal	dog
1930	Jan. 30, 1930–Feb. 16, 1931	metal	horse	1971	Jan. 27, 1971–Feb. 14, 1972	metal	boar
1931	Feb. 17, 1931–Feb. 5, 1932	metal	goat	1972	Feb. 15, 1972–Feb. 2, 1973	water	rat
1932	Feb. 6, 1932–Jan. 25 1933	water	monkey	1973	Feb. 3, 1973–Jan. 22, 1974	water	ox
1933	Jan 26, 1933–Feb. 13, 1934	water	rooster	1974	Jan. 23, 1974–Feb. 10, 1975	wood	tiger
1934	Feb. 14, 1934–Feb 3, 1935	wood	dog	1975	Feb. 11, 1975–Jan. 30, 1976	wood	rabbit
1935	Feb. 4, 1935–Jan. 23, 1936	wood	boar	1976	Jan. 31, 1976–Feb. 17, 1977	fire	dragon
1936	Jan. 24, 1936–Feb 10. 1937	fire	rat	1977	Feb. 18, 1977–Feb. 6, 1978	fire	snake
1937	Feb. 11, 1937–Jan 30, 1938	fire	ox	1978	Feb. 7, 1978–Jan. 27, 1979	earth	horse
1938	Jan. 31, 1938–Feb 18, 1939	earth	tiger	1979	Jan. 28, 1979–Feb. 15, 1980	earth	goat
1939	Feb. 19, 1939–Feb 7, 1940	earth	rabbit	1980	Feb. 16, 1980–Feb. 4, 1981	metal	monkey
1940	Feb. 8, 1940–Jan. 26, 1941	metal	dragon	1981	Feb. 5, 1981–Jan. 24, 1982	metal	rooster
1941	Jan. 27, 1941–Feb. 14, 1942	metal	snake	1982	Jan. 25, 1982–Feb.12, 1983	water	dog
1942	Feb. 15, 1942–Feb 4, 1943	water	horse	1983	Feb. 13, 1983–Feb. 1, 1984	water	boar
1943	Feb, 5, 1943–Jan. 24, 1944	water	goat	1984	Feb. 2, 1984–Feb. 19, 1985	wood	rat
1944	Jan. 25, 1944–Feb. 12, 1945	wood	monkey	1985	Feb. 20, 1985–Feb. 8, 1986	wood	ox
1945	Feb. 13, 1945–Feb. 1, 1946	wood	rooster	1986	Feb. 9, 1986–Jan. 28, 1987	fire	tiger
1946	Feb. 2, 1946–Jan. 21, 1947	fire	dog	1987	Jan. 29, 1987–Feb. 16, 1988	fire	rabbit
1947	Jan. 22, 1947–Feb. 9, 1948	fire	boar	1988	Feb. 17, 1988–Feb. 5, 1989	earth	dragon
1948	Feb. 10, 1948–Jan. 28, 1949	earth	rat	1989	Feb. 6, 1989–Jan. 26, 1990	earth	snake
1949	Jan. 29, 1949–Feb. 16, 1950	earth	ox	1990	Jan. 27, 1990–Feb. 14, 1991	metal	horse
1950	Feb. 17, 1950–Feb. 5, 1951	metal	tiger	1991	Feb. 15, 1991–Feb. 3, 1992	metal	goat
1951	Feb. 6, 1951–Jan. 26, 1952	metal	rabbit	1992	Feb. 4, 1992–Jan. 22, 1993	water	monkey
1952	Jan. 27, 1952–Feb. 13, 1953	water	dragon	1993	Jan. 23, 1993–Feb. 9, 1994	water	rooster
1953	Feb. 14, 1953–Feb. 2, 1954	water	snake	1994	Feb. 10, 1994–Jan. 30, 1995	wood	dog
1954	Feb.2, 1954–Jan 23, 1955	wood	horse	1995	Jan. 31, 1995–Feb. 18, 1996	wood	boar
1955	Jan. 24, 1955–Feb. 11, 1956	wood	goat	1996	Feb. 19, 1996–Feb. 6, 1997	fire	rat
1956	Feb. 12, 1956–Jan. 30, 1957	fire	monkey	1997	Feb. 7, 1997–Jan. 27, 1998	fire	ox
1957	Jan. 31, 1957–Feb. 17, 1958	fire	rooster	1998	Jan. 28, 1998–Feb. 15, 1999	earth	tiger
1958	Feb. 18, 1958–Feb. 7, 1959	earth	dog	1999	Feb. 16, 1999–Feb. 4, 2000	earth	rabbit
1959	Feb. 8, 1959–Jan. 27, 1960	earth	pig	2000	Feb. 5, 2000–Jan. 23, 2001	metal	dragon
1960	Jan. 28, 1960–Feb. 14, 1961	metal	rat	2001	Jan. 24, 2001–Feb. 11, 2002	metal	snake
1961	Feb. 15, 1961–Feb. 4, 1962	metal	ox	2002	Feb. 12, 2002–Jan. 31, 2003	water	horse
1962	Feb. 5, 1962–Jan. 24, 1963	water	tiger	2003	Feb. 1, 2003–Jan. 21, 2004	water	goat
1963	Jan. 25, 1963–Feb. 12, 1964	water	rabbit	2004	Jan. 22, 2004–Feb. 8, 2005	wood	monkey
1964	Feb. 13, 1964–Feb. 1, 1965	wood	dragon	2005	Feb. 9, 2005–Jan. 28, 2006	wood	rooster

ANIMAL SIGNS

THE CREATURES OF THE ZODIAC

If you are a Westerner, this probably sounds familiar: You are sitting in a Chinese restaurant, waiting for your meal to arrive. To amuse yourself, you study your placemat, which is printed with the Chinese zodiac. The Chinese zodiac is composed of 12 animal star signs, similar to the 12 star signs used in Western astrology. However, instead of categorizing you by what month you were born, Chinese zodiac classifies people according to the year they were born. There is one thing, however, that those placemats don't tell you—an important thing, too: The Chinese zodiac does not follow the western calendar.

The Chinese zodiac follows the Chinese calendar, which is a little different from the one Westerners are used to. The years, such as 1966, 1967, 1968, and so on, are the same in both calendars, but instead of starting in January, the Chinese lunar New Year starts between late January and mid-February. What does this mean? Simply that all you January- and February-born diners may have miscalculated your Chinese animal sign. To find out what your correct sign is, turn to page 173. Once you've found out, come back to this page and read your animal's personality profile.

RAT—POPULAR

Persons born in the year of the rat are happy, charming, and very charismatic. Very social, rats enjoy being surrounded by their many friends. Hard-working, detail-oriented, thrifty, and ambitious, rats have excellent business sense and are able to accumulate money easily. If not careful, however, rat people can become greedy and self-obsessed. Rat people often find it difficult not to gossip or criticize others behind their backs. Rats are compatible with dragons, monkeys, and oxen. Rats clash with horses, and rabbits.

OX—METHODICAL

One of the most noticeable traits about oxen is their great calm, even in the face of chaos. Persons born in an ox year are said to be tenacious, bright, hard-working, and logical. Oxen like routine, details, and success—these traits and their great trustworthiness make them valuable employees. Oxen of both sexes are excellent providers, making sure that no one in their immediate or extended family goes without. However, it is important for oxen to practice tolerance and spontaneity for, without these, they can become autocratic and rigid. Oxen are compatible with snakes, roosters, and rats. Oxen clash with tigers and horses.

TIGER—UNPREDICTABLE

Persons born in the year of the tiger are said to be magnetic, romantic, independent, courageous, adventurous, and impulsive. A great lover of life, the tiger has a daring and intense spirit and does what he or she wants, when he or she wants. Although tigers can be very warm, their hunger for adventure can make them reckless, leading them to disregard the feelings of those around them. Tigers must be mindful in order not to become narcissistic, brash, or dangerously possessive of friends and lovers. Tigers are compatible with horses, dragons, dogs, and pigs. Tigers clash with monkeys and snakes.

RABBIT—LUCKY

Sometimes referred to in Chinese astrology as the hare or even the cat, the rabbit is discreet, well-mannered, and gracious. Persons born in the year of the rabbit are said to be talented, affectionate yet shy, and considerate—perhaps it is these solid traits that make the rabbit the most fortunate among the 12 animals. This good fortune extends to the business world, where the rabbit's good judgement and sound advice make him or her a much-sought-after negotiator. Rabbits have a love of home and comfortable living, but must be careful not to become self-indulgent and superficial. Rabbits are compatible with pigs, dragon, and goats. Rabbits clash with roosters, tigers, and rats.

DRAGON—CHARISMATIC

Just like their mythological counterparts, dragon people are colorful, enthusiastic, fiery, energetic, and passionate. These take-charge risk-takers can be counted on to make things happen, whether it is a rally that needs organizing or a dream that wants to be fulfilled. The dragon person has many friends and admirers but can be prone to arrogance if not careful and must be mindful not to let his or her forceful nature become too argumentative, fanatical, or perfectionist. Should this happen, the dragon finds it easy to ask for forgiveness from anyone he or she has offended. Dragons are compatible with rats, monkeys, and pigs. Dragons clash with dogs and dragons.

SNAKE—THINKERS

Those born under the snake sign are blessed with strong innate wisdom and intuition. Snake people are great thinkers, preferring to reflect upon something before forming an opinion. This makes snakes fast learners who rarely make the same mistake twice. Appreciative of fine books, theater, music, food, and wine, the snake has sophisticated tastes and enjoys life's luxuries. Although snakes are endowed with great charm, they can be highly suspicious and skeptical and must work hard to avoid growing paranoid or neurotic with age. It it is the snake's natural tendency to be unforgiving and revenge-seeking. Snakes are compatible with roosters and oxen. Snakes clash with tigers and pigs.

HORSE—FREEDOM-LOVING

Persons born in the year of the horse love freedom—of all sorts. Freedom from routine. Freedom to work his or her own hours. And freedom from anyone intending to rope him or her in. Fortunately, freedom suits the industrious, self-reliant horse, who is able to do several tasks at once. Attractive, friendly, confident, and proud, horses must be careful not to manipulate people with their sex appeal and charm. Because horses are headstrong and don't easily tolerate those who are incapable or of low intelligence, horses must be careful to cultivate understanding and tolerance. Horses are compatible with tigers, dogs, and goats. Horses clash with rats and oxen.

GOAT—SENSITIVE

Often referred to as the sheep, the goat is perceptive, creative, eccentric, and multitalented. These elegant creatures love romance and adoration and are very generous, making them terrific lovers, parents, and pet owners. Goats hate to be pushed into a decision or situation and can become withdrawn and lazy if forced to do something they don't want to do. Due to their sensitive natures, goats can easily become pessimistic and depressed. Fortunately they are also lucky and whenever they encounter a problem, a supportive friend is usually nearby to help. Goats are compatible with rabbits, pigs, and horses. Goats clash with oxen, tigers and roosters.

MONKEY—WILY

The curious monkey will try anything once, repeating a new skill until he or she has mastered it. Cunning, ingenious, and ambitious, the monkey researches what he or she needs to do to become the best in a chosen field, then goes about his or her climb to the top. Failure is not a word in the monkey's vocabulary. Full of self-confidence, monkeys can become overly competitive, self-centered, and untrustworthy if they don't work to curb their self-determination. Monkeys are compatible with rats, dragons, and monkeys. Monkeys clash with horses and pigs.

ROOSTER—METICULOUS

In Chinese astrology, the rooster is often referred to as the cock. Roosters are routine-loving, detail-oriented perfectionists who are known for their precision, money-making skills, list-making, and tidy ways. Brave, intelligent, and enthusiastic, roosters love to travel and learn about new cultures. Unfortunately, the rooster's intelligence can make him or her pretentious and opinionated. If the rooster is not careful, this over-abundance of pride can lead to loneliness. Roosters are compatible with snakes, oxen, and pigs. Roosters clash with goats.

DOG—LOYAL

Persons born in the year of the dog are said to be honest, loyal, generous, dutiful, trustworthy, unprejudiced, and warm-hearted. Dogs are down-to-earth creatures who care more for justice than for money. Indeed, dogs are well-known as people who fight for their principles. However, dog people must be careful not to let their sense of justice turn into self-righteousness. While usually even-tempered, dog people can become mean-spirited and spiteful when wronged. Dogs are compatible with rabbits. Dogs clash with dragons and oxen.

BOAR—NURTURING

Also known as the pig, the boar is a model of sincerity, loyalty, and honor. Generous with their time and resources pigs are genuinely nice people who make sure you are comfortable. Self-sacrificing, slow-to-anger, chivalrous, patient, gallant, good listeners and altruistic, the boar will do anything for anybody. While these traits enable the boar to make strong, lasting friendships, they also make the boar extremely gullible. Boars must be careful not to fall prey to opportunistic acquaintances, hustlers, or con artists. Boars are compatible with dragons, goats, and rabbits. Boars clash with snakes.

FINDING YOUR PERSONAL TRIGRAM

To determine whether you belong to the east group or west group, you must determine your own personal trigram. Start by turning to Chinese Calendar (page 172-173) and finding your correct Chinese birthyear. From there, follow this formula:

FEMALE

1. Add the digits in your birth year. (For instance 1967 would be 1+9+6+7=23.)
2. Divide the sum by 9. (For the year 1967, 23 divided by 9 would be 2, with a remainder of 5.)
3. Add 4 to the remainder in the above equation. (4+5=9)
4. The resulting number represents your personal trigram. To learn more about your personal trigram, turn to The Eight Trigrams (page 34–35) and look for the trigram whose number corresponds to the number you have calculated above.

MALE

1. Add the digits in your birth year. (For instance 1967 would be 1+9+6+7=23.)
2. Divide the sum by 9. (For the year 1967, 23 divided by 9 would be 2, with a remainder of 5.)
3. Subtract the remainder in the above calculation from 11. (11-5=6)
4. The resulting number represents your personal trigram (see page 34–35 to find the trigram that equates with this number).

THE EAST/WEST SYSTEM

While not all feng shui masters use the east/west System, it's a good thing to know. The east/west system uses what you learned about the pa kua to determine your four lucky and your four unlucky directions. It is also used to find out who–you are compatible and incompatible with. Uncovering your chosen directions is not difficult—all you need to do is find out your personal trigram. To do that, first find your personal trigram (on this page).

Got it? Now locate your trigram among those in the Eight Trigrams section on pages 34-35. If you are a chen, sun, kan, or li, you belong to the east group. If you are a chien, kun, ken, or tui, you belong to the west group. True, within the east group there is kan (north) and li (south); and within the west group there is ken (northeast). If you do not want to be terrifically confused, we suggest that you do not think about this too much!

Very generally speaking, if you are a member of the east group, you feel at ease with all eastern directions and other members of the eastern group. If you are a member of the west group, you feel most comfortable with western directions and members of the western group.

THE YELLOW CALENDAR

The Yellow Calendar is a kind of super, multi-use daily calendar, created in the time of the Yellow Emperor. It includes elements from the traditional Chinese calendar, the Western Gregorian calendar, the particular micro-season according to the 24 Season calendar (see page 157), as well as the day's lucky wealth direction, the day's lucky happiness direction, the activities that are best performed on that particular day, and the activities that are best avoided on that particular day.

Seen hanging in Chinese institutions such as banks, some Chinese businesses, and in most Chinese homes, the Yellow Calendar is consulted daily by individuals who are both eager to court auspicious energy and anxious to avoid inauspicious energy. Other people look only to the Yellow Calendar to find the best and worst days to schedule a big event, such as a business's grand opening, a wedding, a home's ground-breaking, an operation, or a vacation.

1. The month according to the Western Gregorian calendar. Here, the month is February.
2. The day according to the Western Gregorian calendar. Here, the day is the 5th. February 5th, 2000—the date shown here—happens to be Chinese spring at the beginning of The Year of the Dragon.
3. A combined Western Gregorian calendar and Chinese solar calendar. This "combined-style" calendar is the type typically seen in modern Chinese homes.
4. The date according to the Chinese lunisolar calendar. Here, it is the first day of the new year.
5. The micro-season according to the 24 Season calendar. In agrarian China, the 24 Season calendar (see page 157) breaks the year into 24 distinct seasons according to weather, precipitation, time of year, and other variables. This calendar is used much like the Farmer's Almanac is used in North America: to help farmers and other people who live off the land know when to prepare their soil, sow seeds, water fields, and harvest crops. This particular day—February 5th according to Western date-keeping—falls at the beginning of the season called Li ch'un, which is the time of year farmers prepare for spring planting.
6. The God of Wealth. This shows the lucky wealth direction for the day and is used by some wealth-seekers to map their daily routes to and from work, school, and other engagements. The God of Wealth direction changes daily; on this particular day, south is the lucky wealth direction.
7. The God of Happiness. This shows the lucky happiness direction for the day and is used much like the God of Wealth information: to

help people map their daily routes in a way that favors the featured direction—on this day it is southeast—in order to bring joy into one's life. The God of Happiness direction changes daily.

8. The Worst Actions. This column tells people what things should not be done on this particular day. The list changes daily and can include information such as going to the doctor, getting married, buying a house, making a big decision, and more. To do one of the listed "worst actions" on that day can bring bad luck in health, wealth, career, relationship, or family matters. People page ahead to calendar entries months away before planning weddings, purchases, business openings, and other events.

9. The Best Actions. This column tells people what things should be done on a particular day. The list changes daily and can include information such as getting a haircut, holding a business's grand opening, throwing a party, making a purchase, and more. Doing one of the listed "best actions" items on this day can bring luck in health, wealth, career, relationship, or family maters. As with the "worst actions," people page ahead before planning major events or occasions.

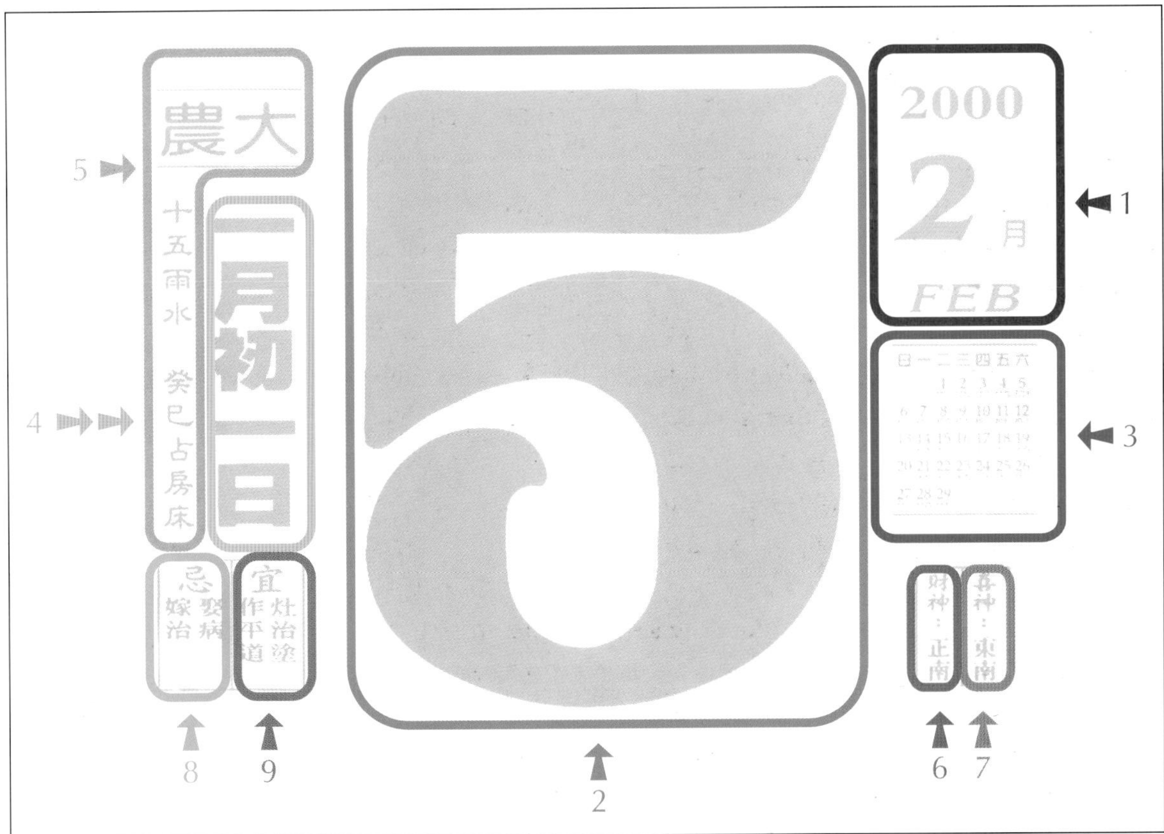

The Yellow Calendar showing Western and Chinese dates, inauspicious and beneficial actions.

CHRONOLOGY OF CHINESE HISTORY

TIME	DEVELOPMENT
Before 4000 B.C.	Yin and Yang concept were perfected The Ho t'u river map with the nine palaces was found The former heaven (or first) pa kua was invented
4000 B.C.	The Yellow Emperor created the five element theory Chinese astrology was developed An early version of the I Ching was thought to be written
2100-1600 B.C.	The five element theory was perfected Chinese astrology was perfected
1600 – 1100 B.C.	The directions north and south were established The latter heaven pa kua, still used today, was developed
1000-780 B.C.	The yin and yang theory was refined to include cosmic, natural and human energy
775 B.C.	Five elements theory applied to geology, geography, biology, and other earth sciences
600-500 B.C.	Yin and yang theory and the five element theory are integrated
580 B.C.	Laozi, founder of Taoism, reputedly born
551 B.C.	Confucius, founder of Confucianism, reputedly born
500 B.C.	The Tao Teh Ching was published, after Laozi's death
494 B.C.	The city Su Zhou is established using early feng shui concepts
286 B.C.	Zhuang Zi, student of Laozi, died. His book, Book of Zhang Zi, is published
300 B.C.	Yellow Emperor's Classic of Internal Medicine, the first book of Chinese medicine, was written
300 B.C.	24 Small Season theory established
200 B.C.	The feng shui placement of Yin Houses (graveyards) grew in importance under the influence of Confucianism
200 B.C-200 A.D.	The compass was invented and perfected Buddhism introduced to China
300 – 400 A.D.	Compass School of feng shui is developed
600 – 800 A.D.	Taoism widely practiced in China Confucianism adhered to among governing classes
880 A.D.	Yang Yun Sung codifies the classic of feng shui

ANCIENT FENG SHUI WISDOM

Feng shui as a practice has been continually refined since its inception, some 6000 years ago. Some modifications occurred as human knowledge increased, while many other changes were prompted by newly-developed technologies. Among the sources both commenting on and instigating changes are the following ancient books:

APPROXIMATE DATE	BOOK
4000 B.C.	An early version of the I Ching, author(s) unknown
200 B.C. – 200 A.D.	Lun Heng, by Wang Chong
200 B.C. – 200 A.D.	Kan Yu Jin Kui, author(s) uknown
200 A.D.	Juan Shi Di Li Zhi Meng, by Guan Ge
300 A.D.	Zang Ching, by Guo Pu
400 A.D.	Yellow Emperor House Classic, by Wang Zheng
800 A.D.	Han Lung Ching, by Yang Yun Sung Yi Lung Ching, by Yang Yun Sung Shih-erh Chang, by Yang Yun Sung Ching Nang Ao Chi, by Yang Yun Sung
1100 A.D.	Nine Star Zhuan Bian, by Liao Yu Xie Tian Ji, by Liao Yu
1300 A.D.	Feng Shui Questions, by Zhu Zhen Hsiang
1500 A.D.	Ren Zi Xu Zhi, by Xue Shan Ji
	Zang Jing Yi, by Liao Xi Yong
	Ti Li Da Cheng, by Yie Jui Sheng
	Ti Li Zheng Zong, by Xiao Ke
	Kan Yu Man Hsing, by Liu Ji
	Water Dragon Ching, by Jiang Bing Jie
	Yang House Ten Book, by Wu Qian Yang House Three Point, by Wu Qian
1700 A.D.	Feng Shui Original Meanings, by Yuan Pei Song

FOR MORE INFORMATION

BOOKS

Brown, Simon, *Essential Feng Shui*, Ward Lock Ltd., 1999.

Choy, Howard, and Henwood, Belinda, *Feng Shui: How to Create Harmony and Balance in Your Living and Working Environment*, Storey Books, 1999.

Dexter, Rosalyn, *Chinese Whispers: Feng Shui*, Rizzoli International, 2000.

Edwards, Jane, *Asian Elemements: Natural Balance in Eastern Design*, Soma Books, 1999.

Eitel, Ernest J., *Feng Shui*, Heian International Publishing Company, 1996.

Elkins, Valmai Howe , *Adventures of a Feng Shui Detective*, Woodley & Watts, 1999.

Kushi, Michio, and Thompson, Gerry, *Feng Shui Astrology for Lovers: How to Improve Love and Relationships*, Sterling Publications, 1998.

Lagatree, Kirsten, and Wong, Angi Ma, *Feng Shui: Arranging Your Home to Change Your Life*, Villard Books, 1996.

Lagatree, Kirsten, *Feng Shui at Work : Arranging Your Work Space to Achieve Peak Performance and Maximum Profit*, Villard Books, 1998.

Lam, Tri, *Encyclopedia of Chinese Astrology*, Lam Inter Media, 1999.

Lin, Jami, *The Essence of Feng Shui: Balancing Your Body, Home and Life with Fragrance*, Hay House, 1998.

Lin, Jami, and Lewison-Singar, Rita, *Feng Shui Anthology: Contemporary Earth Design*, Earth Design, 1997.

Lip, Evelyn, *Environments of Power: A Study of Chinese Architecture*, John Wiley & Sons, 1995.

Lip, Evelyn, *Feng Shui: Layman's Guide to Chinese Geomancy*, Heian Intnternational Publishing Company, 1987.

Rossbach, Sarah, *Feng Shui: The Chinese Art of Placement*, E.P. Dutton, 1995.

Skinner, Stephen, *Feng Shui: The Traditional Oriental Way*, Paragon, 1997.

Thompson, Angel, *Feng Shui: How to Achieve the Most Harmonious Arrangement of Your Home and Office*, St. Martin's Press, 1996.

Too, Lillian, *A Step-by-Step Guide to Enhancing Your Relationships, Health, and Prosperity*, Ballantine Books, 1999.

Too, Lillian, *The Complete Illustrated Guide to Feng Shui for Gardens*, Element, 1999.

Too, Lillian, *The Complete Illustrated Guide to Feng Shui: How to Apply the Secrets of Chinese Wisdom for Health, Wealth and Happiness*, Element, 1996.

Too, Lillian, *The 'Feng Shui Fundamentals' Series*, Element, 1997.

Webster, Richard, *101 Feng Shui Tips for the Home*, Llewellyn Publications. 1998.

Wu, Ying, *Do-It-Yourself Feng Shui: Take Charge of Your Destiny!*, Element, 1998.

Wydra, Nancilee, *Designing Your Own Happiness: A Contemporary Look at Feng Shui*, Heian Intnternational Publishing Company, 1995.

Wydra, Nancilee, *The Book of Cures: 150 Simple Solutions for Health and Happiness in Your Home or Office*, Heian Intnternational Publishing Company, 1998.

WEBSITES

The Art of Placement:
http://www.artofplacement.com

Handilinks:
http://www.handilinks.com/index.htm

Elibrary – Feng Shui:
http://www.elibrary.com

Feng Shui Gallery New York:
http://www.fengshuigallerynewyork.com

World of Feng Shui:
http://www.worldoffengshui.com

GLOSSARY

BUDDHISM: A religion founded in Northern India in the 6th century B.C. by Siddhartha Gautama, who became known as the Buddha (Enlightened One). While there are many different types of Buddhism, Zen Buddhism is the type prevalent in China.

CHEN: One of the eight trigrams found on the pa kua, Chen is represented by two broken yin lines above an unbroken yang line. It denotes decisiveness, sudden, unexpected energy. Located in the east, chen symbolizes the eldest and early spring.

CHI: The universal life force, or energy, that exists in every living and non-living thing. Chi can be auspicious, inauspicious, or benign.

CHIEN: One of the eight trigrams found on the pa kua, Chien is represented by three unbroken yang lines. It denotes strong, persistent energy. Located in the northwest position, it symbolizes the father/ husband—or a business's president or country's ruler. The season Chien represents is the time between late fall and early winter.

CHINESE CALENDAR: Unlike the solar calendar used by most Western cultures, the Chinese calendar is both lunar and solar in nature. The years, such as 1966, 1967, 1968 and so on, are the same in both Western and Chinese calendars, yet instead of starting in January, the Chinese solar New Year starts in February—at a very specific time usually on either the fourth or fifth, depending on the year. The lunar New Year moves between mid-January and mid-February each year.

CONFUCIUS: The Chinese philosopher and teacher who lived during the 5th and 6th centuries B.C. Known as Chiu Kong, Kong the Philosopher, or K'ung-fu'-tse, Confucius emphasized the importance of li (proper behavior), jen (sympathetic attitude) and (hsiao) ancestor worship—all tenets that remain important in China. Feng shui is not closely associated with Confucianism.

DOMINATION CYCLE: The domination cycle is a chaotic cycle of imbalance which weakens and even depletes chi. Sometimes referred to as the destruction cycle, the Chinese believe that this causes environmental imbalances (such as Global Warming) and human illness (such as weakened immune systems).

DRAGON: The mythical creature is among China's most revered symbols. Within feng shui, dragons—including dragon mountains and dragon breath—represent auspiciousness.

EAST GROUP. An element of the East/West System; also known as the East Four Houses. The east four houses are derived from four directions found on the pa kua. They are Li, Kan, Chen, and Sun.

EAST/WEST SYSTEM: A system that uses the pa kua to categorize people according to their auspicious directions. Depending on their time of birth, people fall into either the East Group (East Four Houses) or the West Group (West Four Houses).

FENG SHUI: In ancient China, "feng" meant "wind," and "shui" meant "water." Feng shui is a term referring to the art and science of life-space. Pronounced "fung schway," this ancient Chinese practice is used to balance the energy in those places where we live and work.

FIVE ELEMENTS: Also called the five phases, the five elements are fire, earth, metal, water, and wood. Each element has a specific type of energy. When combined in various combinations, these elements can harmonize or oppose each other.

FU HSI: Known also as Wu of Hsia, this early emperor ruled nearly 5,000 to 6,000 years ago and is believed to be China's first ruler. While there is no concrete evidence he existed, he is credited with developing the eight trigrams now known as Lo Shu. Many scholars also believe Fu Hsi wrote an early version of the I Ching.

HO T'U RIVER MAP: Also called the Yellow River Map, this is a pattern of filled (yang) and unfilled (yin) circles that symbolize the ideal balance of heaven and nature.

I CHING: The philosophical basis of feng shui. Also known as the Yijing or Book of Changes, it is believed to be China's oldest book and is thought to be the first recorded attempt to explain yin and yang.

KAN: One of the eight trigrams found on the pa kua, Kan is represented by an unbroken yang line between two broken yin lines. It symbolizes ambitious, driven, industrious (though sometimes deceitful) chi. Located in the north, kan symbolizes the middle brother. The season kan represents is winter.

KEN: One of the eight trigrams found on the pa kua, Ken is represented by an unbroken yang line above two broken yin lines. It denotes solid, stable, intuitive chi. Located in the northeast, ken symbolizes the youngest son and early spring.

KUN: One of the eight trigrams found on the pa kua, Kun is represented by three broken yin lines. It symbolizes nurturing, receptive chi. Located in the southwest, kun symbolizes the mother. The season kun represents is late summer.

LAOZI: Also called Lao Tzu or Li Erh, Lao Tzu was a philosopher who lived in the late 500s B.C.. He recorded his insights in what became known as the Tao Te Ching (also called the Dao De Jing) and is credited with developing Taoism.

LI: One of the eight trigrams found on the pa kua, Li is represented by a broken yin line between two straight yang lines. It denotes successful, brilliant, warm chi. Located in the south, li symbolizes the middle daughter and summer.

LO P'AN: A type of compass used in feng shui's Compass School. The Lo P'an consists of a south-pointing compass surrounded by the pa kua, astrology information and other details that could help a feng shui practitioner.

LO SHU: Sometimes referred to as Magic Square because it consists of a series of numbers arranged inside a grid. All horizontal, vertical and diagonal rows add up to the same number. It is said that Fu Hsi found the original Lo Shu on a tortoise shell. The Lo Shu is used when determining the Nine Palaces.

NINE PALACES: Known also as the nine floating stars, the flying stars, the purple-white flying palace, the purple-white flying stars, and the purple-white nine stars, the nine palaces referred to in the name are the seven stars of the big dipper constellation, plus two believed-to-be-invisible companion stars. The system is used to determine auspicious and inauspicious times during any given period for both humans and buildings.

PA KUA: An octagon surrounded by the eight trigrams of the I Ching and representing the eight compass directions. With one arrangement of triagrams it has a mirror or yin-yang symbol in its center and is used as a symbol of protection. With another arrangement it is used to determine a person's most auspicious and inauspicious directions and locations.

POISON ARROW: Known also as shar, this is negative energy that carries misfortune. Poison arrows travel in straight lines and are created when any type of straight line or corner points toward a house.

PRODUCTIVE CYCLE: Known also as the birth cycle, the productive cycle is a positive, productive cycle in which each of the elements—fire, earth, metal, water, wood—helps create the element that follows it. The balanced progression of the productive cycle represents harmony and creation.

CHI KUNG: Originally devised by early Taoists, chi kung is a form of energy work designed to help humans attract and control chi within the body.

REDUCTIVE CYCLE: The reductive cycle is a healing cycle used to remedy the chaos created by the domination cycle of the 5 elements. A practical application of the reductive cycle would be a person has too much of one element, say water; adding wood to help absorb the water's effect.

COMPASS SCHOOL: A feng shui ideology interested in the best locations, directions, and situations for each individual. Developed in the Fujian province, it is rooted in the idea that each of the eight cardinal directions (north, northwest, east, southeast, south, southwest, west, northwest) exert a different energy. Also called Li Fa, it is a mathematical, method that uses direction, astronomy, astrology, and numerology.

FORM SCHOOL: A feng shui ideology first used to orient tombs. Later, it was used to orient homes according to surrounding geography, water availability and typical weather patterns. An intuitive approach to feng shui, Form School uses analysis, common sense and perception to create lucky placements. Also called Hsing Fa, it was formed in Jiang Xi province. It is the oldest feng shui system, dating back before the Chin dynasty (300 A.D.).

SHAR: See Poison Arrow.

SUN: One of the eight trigrams on the pa kua, Sun is represented by two unbroken yang lines above a broken yin line. It denotes wholeness, a good and sound mind and great inner strength. Located in the southeast, Sun symbolizes the eldest daughter and late spring or early summer.

TAOISM: Based on teachings of the Tao, this ancient religion is rooted in nature worship. A basic tenet of Taoism is the order and harmony of nature, which is considered more stable and enduring than the power of any human government or civilized institutions. Early Taoists were especially enthusiastic supporters of wu wei. Roughly translated as "no action", this approach taught that art and life followed the creative path of nature—not the values of human society.

TUI: One of the eight trigrams on the pa kua, Tui is represented by a broken yin line above two unbroken yang lines. It denotes happy, satisfied chi. Located in the west, tui symbolizes the youngest and autumn.

TORTOISE: Turtles and tortoises are symbols of longevity and quiet strength in China. The eight trigrams were derived from a diagram now known as Lo Shu, which Fu Hsi found on the shell of a tortoise.

TRIGRAM: The pa kua uses eight trigrams. A trigram is a symbol that features a combination of three broken or unbroken lines. The unbroken line represents yang, while the broken line represents yin.

WEST GROUP: An element of the East/West System; also known as the Four House System. The west four houses are derived from four directions found on the pa kua. They are chien, kun, ken, and tui.

YIN AND YANG: While the concept may have been in China much longer, the term "yin and yang" was not created until late in the Zhou dynasty by philosophers looking for a way to describe the way opposites depended on each other. According to these ancient philosophers, yin and yang is an always-changing combination. Day gives way to night, something hot can grow cold, someone outgoing can become self-protective, the living eventually die. According to Chinese thought, this constant flux is a good thing. It is what creates chi or the life giving force of the universe.

ZHOUYI: Also called the Changes of Zhou, this ancient book was written during the Zhou dynasty (1122-255 B.C.). Later called the I Ching.

INDEX

ACKNOWLEDGMENTS

AUTHOR'S ACKNOWLEDGMENTS

Bringing the ancient wisdom of the Chinese culture to America is a passion through which I have found many rewards. I would never have been able to do this without the help and encouragement of my American friends. Some of those who immediately come to mind are David Paul Filosa, Rodney Martin, Bill Motzing, and Kenny Hui. Also, I would like to express my appreciation to the Allan family who has been very supportive to me. Joseph and Mari (my American parents), Jody and Chris all encouraged me to follow the path that I am on right now.

Studying architecture in China gave me a core foundation in life-space design as well as revealed the mystical aspects of feng shui to me. I would like to thank all the professors and masters in China who have helped me discover the verifiable benefits of feng shui that I am now teaching. I also would like to thank my best friend Ying Chen in Beijing, who has helped me search for valuable information in Asia.

I am also thankful to have worked with the following people at DK Publishing: LaVonne Carlson, whose commitment to bring the knowledge of the East to the West is highly commendable; Stephanie Pederson, for her great efforts in understanding the ancient Chinese arts and presenting them to the West; Barbara Berger for her hours of searching among thousands of pictures and tireless coordinating for the project; Tina Vaughan, for her wonderful vision of a delicate presentation for the whole book; Dirk Kaufman, for his talented cover design and his generous help at the beginning; Scott Meola, for his patience and efforts for the fine project that he delivered in such a short time; and Mandy Earey, for her help with the final touches. I also want to thank other people who have helped this project in some way: Andrew Sicco, Gregor Hall, Jill Bunyan, and Christo.

PUBLISHER'S ACKNOWLEDGMENTS

DK Publishing, Inc., would like to thank the following people their invaluable help: Zaihong Sara Shen for her visionary explication of feng shui; Stephen Skinner at Feng Shui for Modern Living magazine for his insightful contribution; Scott Meola for his beautiful design; Claire Legemah for her thoughtful design development; Dirk Kaufman for his exquisite jacket design; Mandy Earey for overseeing the complex design process, and Michelle Baxter, Jill Bunyan, and Megan Clayton for their design and DTP expertise. For their unflagging assistance in supplying photographic material we would like to thank Martin Copeland and Mark Dennis at the DK Picture Library, and Mariana Sonnenberg and Louise Thomas at ilumi. Special thanks go to Stephanie Pedersen for her role in helping to develop the manuscript, Nanette Cardon at IRIS for her indexing wizardry, and Soo Jin Park for her incredible illustrations. And we are grateful to assistant picture editor Laarnie Ragaza and assistant designer Jonathan Bennett.

PICTURE CREDITS

Additional Photography
Max Alexander, Peter Anderson, Philip Blenkinsop, Paul Bricknell, Geoff Brightling, Demetrio Carrasco, Andy Crawford, Michael Crockett, Geoff Dann, Michael Dent, Philip Dowell, Mike Dunning, Simone End, Philip Enticknap, David Exton, Jake Fitzjones, Neil Fletcher and Matthew Ward, Peter Gathercole, Steve Gorton, David Gower, John Heseltine, Alan Hills, Jacqui Hurst, Stuart Isett, Colin Keates, Barnabas Kindersley, Dave King, Eddie Lawrence, Neil Lukas, Michael Moran, James Morrell, Roger Moss, David Murray, Ian O'Leary, Roger Phillips, Nick Pope, Jonathan Potter, Rob Reichenfeld, Kim Sayer, Jules Selmes and Debi Treloar, Roger Stewart, Clive Streeter, Linda Whitwam, Matthew Ward, Peter Wilson, Stephen Whitehorn, Steven Wooster

Additional picture research by ilumi

t = top; b = bottom; l = left; r = right; c = center

Illustrations by Soo Jin Park:
14br, 24tr, 26br, 27tl, 30b, 31tl, 33t, 34, 35, 37t, 38cr, 39cl, 39cr, 41b, 48bl, 50bl, 51tl, 52bl, 53cl, 53bl, 55br, 58cl, 63bl, 65bl, 67tr, 69l, 74cr, 85, 86b, 87b, 88r, 91, 92, 93b, 98, 108c, 109c, 113tl, 114br, 119r, 120c, 121c, 138br, 140t, 141bl, 144tr, 145cl, 145br, 148c, 149c, 150c, 151c, 152c, 153c, 155tr, 160br, 181b

The publishers would like to thank the following for their kind permission to reproduce the photographs:
Chris Allen, backflap;**Ashmolean Museum** 166br; **Bodleian Library, University of Oxford, Oxford** SINICA 2728 7tr; **The Art Archive: Freer Gallery of Art** 12–13; **Bodleian Library, University of Oxford** SINICA 2728 15tr; **The Bridgeman Art Library, London / New York: Bibliothèque Nationale, Paris, France** 20r; **British Museum** 9tl, 25 tl (dragon and tiger), 79br (Shinto God and Buddha), 111tr, 167br; **Collection des indiennes, Paris** 52tr; **Peter Cook/Architects: Fiona McLean** 49tl, 49tr; **Peter Cook/Michael Winter** 59cl, 109tl; **Tim Daly** 58 tr; **Brian Cosgrove** 156tr, 156bcr (snow), 156br; **Gables** 38bc, 161br; **Galaxy Picture Library: Robin Scagell** 41c; **The Garden Picture Library: John Neubauer** 105t, 126br; **Chris Gascoigne/Alan Power Architects** 73tr; **Chris Gascoigne/Simon Condor Associates** 49tr; **Glasgow Museum** 79br (Confucian ancestor scroll, Christian cross, and Islamic prayer beads); **The Interior Archive: Jonathan Pilkington / Owner: Max Rotheston** 102bl; **IPC Syndication: Homes and Gardens/John Mason** 69br; **Laura Ashley** 70br; **Jewish Museum** 79br (Mezuzah); **Peter James Kindersley** 94bl, 99cr (brick), 113tr; **Mainstream: Ray Main** 44–45, 57tr, 64bl, 72bl; **Norman McGrath** 123bl; **Stephen Oliver** 140bl; **Oriental Museum, Durham University, UK** 16, 79br (Shiva); **Pitt Rivers Museum** 23cl; **© Paul Redman/Stone 2000** 74br; **Royal Albert Memorial/David Garner** 153tr; **Royal Asiatic Society, London, UK** 25cl (turtle); **Science Museum** 167tr; **Neil Setchfield** 81tr. 95bl; **View: Peter Cook/Conran Tugman** 100bl; **Fritz von der Schulenburg/Designer: Barefoot Elegance** 43; **Steven Wooster** 93tr.